MW01474417

Copyright ©2022
All rights reserved. Written permission must be secured from the author to reproduce any part of the book.

Printed in the United States of America

ISBN: 978-1-0881-2512-0

10 9 8 7 6 5 4 3 2 1

EMPIRE PUBLISHING
www.empirebookpublishing.com

Contents

INTRODUCTION 1
CHAPTER 1: FIND OUT WHO YOU ARE 4
    Seek Within: 4
    Key Questions: 6
    Your Past 8
    Your Present 8
    Your Future 8
    Your Virtues and Traits 9
    Your Gifts and Talents: 10
        The Gift of Wisdom: 11
        The Gift of Knowledge and Intelligence 13
        The Gift of Faith 16
        The Gift of Healing 18
        The Gift of Making Miracles 19
        The Gift of Prophecy 20
        The Gift of Acknowledgement 22
        The Gift of Service: 23
        Help or Support 24
CHAPTER 2: DISCOVER YOUR DREAMS, PROJECTS, AND PRIORITIES: 28
    Why is it important to know what we want? 28
    Your Dreams 28
    Your Goals 29
    Short-Term Goals 30

- Long-Term Goals 30
- Set Your Priorities in Order.. 32
- Spiritual Health.. 33
- Mental and Physical Health 34
- Mental/Emotional Health 34
- Family.. 35
- Finances... 36

CHAPTER 3: YOUR SPIRITUAL LIFE 38
- Why is it important to follow a spiritual life? 38
- Seeking from God with a True Heart 38
- Our role in front of others 39
- Happy are those who have a Humble Heart.................... 41
- Patience and Trust... 44
- Keep an Unbreakable Faith... 45
- How do we embrace Lord's lessons?................................. 49
- Wisdom... 51
- The Storm.. 53
- Blessings and Obligations 54

CHAPTER 4: PHYSICAL, EMOTIONAL AND MENTAL HEALTH.. 57
- Your Physical Health 57
- Your Emotional Health 58
- Your Mental Health 60

CHAPTER 5: YOUR PERSONAL RELATIONSHIPS 61
- The Mirror We Should Take a Look On 61
- Your Couple's Relationship 62

Love 62

Respect 67

Attention: 67

Words of Affirmation and Support 68

Presents 69

Comprehension 69

Sexual Intimacy 70

Bed and Sex 71

Kids 74

Social and Business Relationships 75

CHAPTER 6: YOUR FINANCIAL GOALS 78

Your pattern for money 78

Your Income 81

What is the first thing you should know? 82

How to Create Goals 83

How to Manage Your Finances 87

Development of a Financial Plan 88

CHAPTER 7: HOW AM I? 92

Your Character 92

Your Attitude 93

Your Self-Esteem 94

Your Optimism 95

CHAPTER 8: PAY THE PRICE FOR SUCCESS 97

Commit Yourself to Success 97

The Cost of Change 98

The Cost of Regret 100
Are you ready to make the change? Let's begin! 100
Contrast between Disobedience and Obedience 101
Love 103
Procrastination 104
Commit to Action 106
Faith 106
Attitude 107
Fear: 107
Pessimism 108
Be an Optimist 109
Impatience Against Patience: 109
Discipline 110
Persistence 110
The Price of Time 111
The Price of Money 112
The Price of Training and Knowledge 112
The Price of Your Dream 113
CONCLUSION 114

Questions and Answers for a Better Life

The objective of the book "Questions and answers for a better life", is to provide advice, in order to achieve happiness and reach personal success, seeking to improve our spiritual, physical, emotional, familiar and economical living standards. In no way does it intend to substitute the help from qualified professionals regarding the personal situation that any reader may be going through in any of the aforementioned matters. Therefore, the author of this book is not responsible for any loss or risk resulting, directly or indirectly, from the use or implementation of the content of the book.

INTRODUCTION

In the following pages, I'll be talking about my own experience and about what has worked for me. The ideas that I'm sharing in this book are not true or false, right or wrong; they just reflect my own results, as well as the amazing results that I've seen in the life of others who have used the principles that are being suggested.

When you read this book, don't let your eyes see the words only. Use the contents that are present here and put them into practice, as your life and the life of your family, as well as your future, may change dramatically as long as you follow the suggested principles. Study them and apply them as if your life and the life of your family depends on it. Begin to put them into practice, give them time, and you will find out that they are truly useful and will result very handy for you.

If some of these principles seem like they are very simple, inefficient, or unrealistic, you have all the right to discard them. But, I can assure you that they do work. I know, also, that this book will provide you with the necessary tools for you to move forward, be happy, and reach the success you have always longed for.

It is very important that you understand the value and importance that each of these areas has for you. If your subconscious doesn't know exactly what it wants, nothing that you learn, and nothing that you do will change your situation. You must know what success means to you at each of these areas, as clear and precise ideas will deliver clear and precise results.

You will understand how does the influence of our background, through our parents, friends, family or social environment around us, has shaped our thoughts, and how this influence has led us to take detrimental action and create habits. I will explain how each one of us has been conditioned to think and act, whether it is regarding happiness or personal and financial success, as well as present the consequences it has had for each one of us.

We will review the difference between how does successful and unsuccessful people think, so that you can change your attitude towards it and create effective changes on yourself. I will use key strategies so that you can correct your mental pattern and learn new steps that will help you to increase your knowledge for achieving your desired success.

You will begin to use statements which will help you to change your current way of thinking, which is not helping you, for new prosperity thoughts. This refocused way of thinking will lead your actions and, therefore, will determine your results. If you think the way that successful people think, and do what they do ¿Don't you think you will also be successful?

Dedicate yourself into learning all that you can about the psychological operation of the mind, mainly on success psychology, as every man and woman that stands out in their goals think in a very different way from others. If you want to get to a superior level of your life, you have to be willing to surpass the limits of your thoughts, to the point where you can change the way you act, so that you can then embrace new growth and prosperity habits.

One thing is for sure, you will have to be brutally honest with yourself and have no excuse, while being humble of heart.

We find several passages on humbleness on the bible:

> *Ephesians 4:2*
>
> *2. Be completely humble and gentle; be patient, bearing with one another in love.*
>
> *Peter 5:6*
>
> *6. Humble yourselves, therefore, under God's mighty hand, that he may lift you up in due time.*
>
> *Philippians 2:3*
>
> *3. Do nothing out of selfish ambition or vain conceit. Rather, in humility value others above yourselves.*
>
> *Proverbs 29:23*
>
> *23. A man's pride will bring him low, But a humble spirit will obtain honor.*

If we truly want to accomplish our dreams and projects, we must acknowledge that God is our Creator, and that nothing is impossible for Him. Also, we must be humble in order to understand that His timing is perfect. Therefore, I recommend that you follow this advice and accept that if you really want changes in your life, you have to modify your narrowed way of thinking and acting. Otherwise, you may elude your responsibilities, but not your outcomes.

CHAPTER 1
FIND OUT WHO YOU ARE

Seek Within:

At some point in our lives, we have all known or guessed our reason for being, living and feeling, those things that give our life meaning. But, as time goes by, we've lost ourselves somewhere along the way, losing our reason for being, and at the same time, our objectives. We have lived a life full of commitments and duties that have distanced us from our environment and we have lost our purpose in the process. If we want to take control of our existence, we must do as follows:

The first thing is to halt. Stop for a moment and ask yourself:

Who Am I? And you will discover the being living within yourself.

How do you see yourself? So that you know who you truly are.

What are my virtues and traits, my values and principles? So that you find out what you are truly made of, those things that give your life value.

What is my purpose in life? That way you will find out why where you created.

What are the most important things for me? So that you find out your priorities, those things that matter to you and that give your life meaning.

What are your dreams and projects? For you to find out what you want to accomplish and posses, as well as those things that you enjoy doing.

In order to be able to be, feel and live what you truly are, you got to give your life meaning. This can be accomplished through your values and principles, combined with your virtues and traits. This set of positive features that you possess will lead you to your **purpose** and, at the same time, will help you to find once again the dreams and projects that give your existence meaning, with the purpose of discovering what God created you for.

It is very important that you stop for an instant so that you can start meditating about what I've said. I know that we are living at a very fast pace and that plenty of times we don't have the time required to do so. But if we want to change the direction and fate of our lives, we have to do it, while acknowledging that we are going to change the fate of our loved ones for the generations to come.

If we really want to achieve the desired happiness and success at any area that we are developing on, we first have to find ourselves and discover who we really are on the inside. Seek within and find the being living inside you. Then you will find your purpose in life, your gifts and talents, as well as your virtues and traits. It is through this discovery you will begin to plant the seeds of abundance. Your thoughts, decisions and actions will no longer be the same and will be built towards the things that have true value and that matter to you.

We all wish to enjoy good spiritual, physical, emotional, familiar and economical health. But, in order to achieve that, we must first discover what *it* means and the importance that

each one of those priorities has for us. To acknowledge our true self will help us to discover our virtues and traits, and at the same time, we will discover our dreams and projects and will recognize our strengths and weaknesses, so that we can later address them. Otherwise, we will spend all of our life trying to achieve our objectives, not knowing that joy, success and happiness is not in the outside, but within ourselves, so that we can later reflect it on the outside.

Most of us live so busy that we don't get time to discover those things that truly matter in our lives. Our own virtues and traits, gifts and talents, and even our strengths and weaknesses, are characteristics that we can't see, invisible features, but that turn out to be far more important than the visible ones, as we are composed by a combination of them. If you are reading this book, it is because you want to grow, and you know that something in you doesn't quite fit right, and that you need a change in your life.

Key Questions:

Who am I?

Discover the being living inside you:

Why don't we start at the beginning? Do you remember when you were just a child and you felt free of thinking and dreaming about all that was possible, and all that life had to offer? What has happened in time? Where are all those dreams and projects? Where have you locked them away?

If we want to feel, once again, what we felt when we were kids, we need to go back to being kids again. In the Bible, Jesus said to Nicodemus that in order to see and enter the Kingdom of God we must first be reborn in spirit. John (3:2-8)

> *2. Rabbi, we know that you are a teacher come from God; for no one can do these signs that You do unless God is with him.*
>
> *3. Jesus answered and said to him: "Most assuredly, I say to you, unless one is born again, he cannot see the kingdom of God."*
>
> *4. Nicodemus said to Him, "How can a man be born when he is old? Can he enter a second time into his mother's womb and be born?"*
>
> *5. Jesus answered, "Most assuredly, I say to you, unless one is born of water and the Spirit, he cannot enter the kingdom of God.*
>
> *6. That which is born of the Spirit is spirit.*
>
> *7. Do not marvel that I said to you, 'you must be born again'.*
>
> *8. The wind blows where it wishes, and you hear the sound of it, but you cannot tell where it comes from and where it goes. So is everyone who is born of the Spirit."*

What does Jesus mean with being born again? That you have to leave all preconceptions that everyone else has imposed on you and which you have created on yourself so that you believe more in Him. Write everything you can about you and your past, your present, and your future, so that you can refocus. Be born again in the spirit of God as you once did, when you were only a little kid with no preconceptions.

Your Past

It helps you to find yourself when you were only a little boy/girl and lived without concerns. At that moment you saw life in a different way, full of possibilities and opportunities.

Your Present

Is your present consistent with your past? Are you giving the best of you in order to fulfill your dreams and projects? Or, have you been distracted by the situations around you, to the point where you don't know who you are, where you are and where you're going to?

3: Your Future

How do you picture yourself? Is your past and present consistent with your virtues and traits? If so, I congratulate you, as you are on the right path, and I wish you all the best. But if you are not, what are you doing or what will you do in order to change your situation?

This exercise will allow you to reach at the deepest of your being in order to discover your life purpose. Who do you really are? What are those things you like? Those things that make you feel special? Those things that make you feel connected with your inner world, with the exterior and with the nature as well as with your loved ones? Discover that what makes you feel unique. Think about all that makes you feel like yourself, alive and full of life. Through this exercise you will discover what are the things that really make you passionate. This is a great opportunity for you to start doing the things that you enjoy and that you were created for.

Your Virtues and Traits

On one hand, a virtue is a strong willingness to carry out good deeds. On the other hand, traits are those positive characteristics that we possess and which define us as a person. They are beneficial ways to think and act which enable us to make and take certain actions at difficult times, turning them into favorable situations. Those who develop their traits and virtues are wise in their way forward; they learn and move on steady and with confidence. Those people who strengthen their traits can see further than those who let them come to a standstill. Their virtues give them strength and courage to act with efficiency and integrity.

Each one of us possess virtues and traits. Even if you think you don't, I am telling you, you do, we all do. Maybe you haven't taken the time to discover them, but once you do, you will find meaning in your life. When you discover your virtues and traits as well as your gifts and talents, and put them into good practice, you will have planted an abundance seed in you, which will last for generations to come.

I am truly telling you, if you spend a moment of your time discovering your virtues and traits, as well as your gifts and talents, through them you will discover your life's purpose and what you were created for, The moment you discover them, I assure you, that you will stop hanging around with chickens and will start flying along with eagles.

Discover what you were created for, through the gifts and talents that God has given you:

Your Gifts and Talents:

Gifts are a present that we receive through the Holy Spirit, which help us to obtain the grace of God so that we can bear the spiritual and personal life with wisdom and holiness.

God has placed gifts and talents in each one of us, giving each one different gifts according to our ability. We must use these gifts for the benefit of everyone, thus creating a strong community that acknowledges the grace of God. It is our duty and commitment to discover and develop the already received gifts in order to make the world we live in a better place. Your gifts are useful for adding value to others and, at the same time, for the honor and glory of the Lord, by doing the things that He has created you for.

When we develop our talents, we get on the path of achieving the perfection of the already received gifts. These gifts and talents have been delivered to us according to our ability and our personal and spiritual blessings depend on them. Once received, only you can make them come alive. No one else can do that for you.

In the bible, Corinthians (12: 4-11, 28), we can find some of the **gifts** that we have received through the Holy Spirit:

---

4. There are different kinds of spiritual gifts, but the same Spirit is the source of them all.

5. There are different kinds of service, but we serve the same Lord.

6. God works in different ways, but it is the same God who does the work in all of us.

> *7. A spiritual gift is given to each of us so we can help each other.*
>
> *8. To one person the Spirit gives the ability to give wise advice; to another the same Spirit gives a message of special knowledge*
>
> *9. The same Spirit gives great faith to another, and to someone else the one Spirit gives the gift of healing*
>
> *10. He gives one person the power to perform miracles, and another the ability to prophesy. He gives someone else the ability to distinguish whether a message is from the Spirit of God or from another spirit. Still another person is given the ability to speak in unknown languages, while another is given the ability to interpret what is being said*
>
> *11. It is the one and only Spirit who distributes all these gifts. He alone decides which gift each person should have.*
>
> *28. And God has appointed in the church first apostles, second prophets, third teachers, then miracles, then gifts of healing, helping, guidance and administrating, and various kinds of languages.*

The Gift of Wisdom: Wisdom (1:1-15)

> *1. Love uprightness you who are rulers on earth, be properly disposed towards the Lord and seek him in simplicity of heart;*
>
> *2. for he will be found by those who do not put him to the test, revealing himself to those who do not mistrust him.*

3. *Know that perverse thoughts, however, separate people from God, and power, when put to the test, confounds the stupid.*

4. *Wisdom will never enter the soul of a wrong-doer, nor dwell in a body enslaved to sin;*

5. *for the holy spirit of instruction flees deceitfulness, recoils from unintelligent thoughts, is thwarted by the onset of vice.*

6. *Wisdom is a spirit friendly to humanity, though she will not let a blasphemer's words go unpunished; since God observes the very soul and accurately surveys the heart, listening to every word.*

7. *For the spirit of the Lord fills the world, and that which holds everything together knows every word said.*

8. *No one who speaks what is wrong will go undetected, nor will avenging Justice pass by such a one.*

9. *For the schemes of the godless will be examined, and a report of his words will reach the Lord to convict him of his crimes.*

10. *There is a jealous ear that overhears everything, not even a murmur of complaint escapes it.*

11. *So beware of uttering frivolous complaints, restrain your tongue from finding fault; even what is said in secret has repercussions, and a lying mouth deals death to the soul.*

12. *Do not court death by the errors of your ways, nor invite destruction through the work of your hands.*

13. *For God did not make Death, he takes no pleasure in destroying the living.*

> *14. To exist -- for this he created all things; the creatures of the world have health in them, in them is no fatal poison. Earth is not subjected to death*
>
> *15. for uprightness is immortal.*

If you lack wisdom, ask the Lord to give you wisdom, do not ask for intelligence, as intelligence is humane while wisdom is divine. Intelligence is usually for your own benefit; while wisdom is for the benefit of all, for everyone. Even if the intelligent can identify right from wrong, fare from unfair, he will usually end up seeking or choosing based on his own interest, which sometimes is not the right thing to do, and will lead us into doing inappropriate things.

However, wisdom is divine and acknowledges the difference between right and wrong, fare and unfair and does the right thing. It is about doing the right thing according to Gods will in every situation. Through wisdom we support ourselves on a divine knowledge that guides us through the path of goodness, therefore building a dignified and prosperous life. If you are lacking wisdom, ask the Lord to give it to you, as wisdom covers all.

The Gift of Knowledge and Intelligence
Sirach (6: 18-37)

> *18. " My child, from your youth choose discipline; and when you have gray hair you will find wisdom.*

18. " My child, from your youth choose discipline; and when you have gray hair you will find wisdom.

19. As though plowing and sowing, draw close to her; then wait for her bountiful crops. For in cultivating her you will work but little, and soon you will eat her fruit.

20. Wisdom is rough ground to the fool! The stupid cannot abide her.

21. She will be like a burdensome stone to them, and they will not delay in casting her aside.

22. For discipline* is like her name, she is not accessible to many.

23. Listen, my child, and take my advice; do not refuse my counsel.

24. Put your feet into her fetters, and your neck under her yoke.

25. Bend your shoulders and carry her and do not be irked at her bonds.

26. With all your soul draw close to her; and with all your strength keep her ways.

27. Inquire and search, seek and find; when you get hold of her, do not let her go.

28. Thus at last you will find rest in her, and she will become your joy.

29. Her fetters will be a place of strength; her snare, a robe of spun gold.

30. Her yoke will be a gold ornament; her bonds, a purple cord.

31. You will wear her as a robe of glory, and bear her as a splendid crown.

32. If you wish, my son, you can be wise; if you apply yourself, you can be shrewd.

33. If you are willing to listen, you can learn; if you pay attention, you can be instructed.

34. Stand in the company of the elders; stay close to whoever is wise.

35. Be eager to hear every discourse; let no insightful saying escape you.

36. If you see the intelligent, seek them out; let your feet wear away their doorsteps!

37. Reflect on the law of the Most High, and let his commandments be your constant study. Then he will enlighten your mind, and make you wise as you desire.

The Lord wises for you to learn everything you can on heaven, earth and everything within your reach regarding his creations, as only then, you will reach a mental and spiritual capacity that will help you to make better decisions. Therefore, it is important to obtain knowledge, using studies as mean to receive the blessings that the Lord has for us, not forgetting to thank Him along the way. Otherwise, we will lose track and will never arrive to the truth. This is described in certain lines of Wisdom (3:7-12)

> *7. In the time of their visitation they will shine forth, and will run like sparks through the stubble.*
>
> *8. They will govern nations and rule over peoples, and the Lord will reign over them forever.*
>
> *9. Those who trust in him will understand truth, and the faithful will abide with him in love,*
>
> *10. But the ungodly will be punished as their reasoning deserves, those who disregarded the righteous*
>
> *and rebelled against the Lord;*
>
> *11. for those who despise wisdom and instruction are miserable. Their hope is vain, their labors are unprofitable, and their works are useless.*
>
> *12. Their wives are foolish, and their children evil; their offspring are accursed.*

The one that is not dedicated to learning, can't grow. The one that doesn't read doesn't grow and the one that doesn't grow; lives a life, his own life, a life full of limitations and shortness due to a lack of information and knowledge. Also, his woman and children will suffer the consequences of his actions as the one that behaves that way cannot give what he doesn't have and can't teach what doesn't know.

The Gift of Faith

Faith means believing in God's plan, as He is in control and will guide us through the path of goodness. Is trusting God, in order to be enlightened by Him. Through faith we find a world of possibilities for healing our sorrows, healing our

wounds, covering our necessities and achieving our dreams and projects. Faith means believing in order to be able to see. Everyone who believes and has faith in the Lord can take over the world, and this is a great victory. Faith means believing in what you expect, even when you can't see it, but if you believe, then you will see it, as explained in Mark (16: 16-18).

> *16. The one who believes and is baptized will be saved; but the one who does not believe will be condemned.*
>
> *17. And these signs will accompany those who believe: by using my name they will cast out demons; they will speak in new tongues;*
>
> *18. they will pick up snakes in their hands, and if they drink any deadly thing, it will not hurt them; they will lay their hands on the sick, and they will recover."*

God has given us gifts and talents, wisdom and knowledge so that we put them into action, and it is by faith that we will get to see the grace of God poured over us. *Today, we have doctors that are capable of healing our diseases. They have discovered the gifts of healing inside them, and, through their faith, they have set his plan in motion for becoming doctors, until they get to be trained for healing our diseases. The same has happened with all those people achieving and reaching their dreams and projects. They have believed in their dreams and initiated a plan for turning those dreams into reality. You can do the same thing, if you believe and trust the Lord.*

The Gift of Healing

God stated that he would give health to its people, that he would free us from diseases or plagues. Precisely, the New Testament mentions, among other miracles, the healing of Matthew, the paralytic (9: 6-7):

> *6. But so that you may know that the Son of Man has authority on earth to forgive sins" —he then said to the paralytic— "Stand up, take your bed and go to your home."*
>
> *7. And he stood up and went to his home.*

Later, it also presents the healing of two blind men: Matthew (20: 29-34):

> *29. As they were leaving Jericho, a large crowd followed him.*
>
> *30. There were two blind men sitting by the roadside. When they heard that Jesus was passing by, they shouted, "Lord,[h] have mercy on us, Son of David!"*
>
> *31. The crowd sternly ordered them to be quiet; but they shouted even more loudly, "Have mercy on us, Lord, Son of David!"*
>
> *32. Jesus stood still and called them, saying, "What do you want me to do for you?"*
>
> *33. They said to him, "Lord, let our eyes be opened."*
>
> *34. Moved with compassion, Jesus touched their eyes. Immediately they regained their sight and followed him.*

On the mentioned statements we find a great meaning, as we can associate both cases to the blindness that won't let us see our possibilities and to the paralysis that stops us from moving forward on the search for our goals.

As people of God, we must listen to His voice, act in justice and live in obedience of his commands. How many troubles will we avoid by doing so?

We, at our daily activities, have lots to do regarding this delicate task, with our actions and our example. Even a small gesture of consolation can lead to someone else's healing.

The Gift of Making Miracles John (11:38-44)

38. Then Jesus, again greatly disturbed, came to the tomb. It was a cave, and a stone was lying against it.

39. Jesus said, "Take away the stone." Martha, the sister of the dead man, said to him, "Lord, already there is a stench because he has been dead four days."

40. Jesus said to her, "Did I not tell you that if you believed, you would see the glory of God?"

41. So they took away the stone. And Jesus looked upward and said, "Father, I thank you for having heard me.

42. I knew that you always hear me, but I have said this for the sake of the crowd standing here, so that they may believe that you sent me."

43. When he had said this, he cried with a loud voice, "Lazarus, come out!"

> 44. The dead man came out, his hands and feet bound with strips of cloth, and his face wrapped in a cloth. Jesus said to them, "Unbind him, and let him go."

Miracles are God's intervention for suspending natural laws and putting his plans into motion. The Lord uses us as instruments to manifest his mercy towards us, through faith and received gifts. With our church in Christ, we must ask the Lord to give us the gift of making miracles in order to manifest his will in such a way that *miracles are* for His honor and glory through us. This is what Jesus did when he left the apostles as his representatives, so that they could continue his work as we see it in Mark 16: 19-20:

> 19. So then the Lord Jesus, after he had spoken to them, was taken up into heaven and sat down at the right hand of God.
>
> 20. And they went out and proclaimed the good news everywhere, while the Lord worked with them and confirmed the message by the signs that accompanied it.

The Gift of Prophecy

It is the power of revealing secrets within a dream or revelation. People that have the gift of prophecy, visualize what could have happened in the past or could happen in the future. At the sacred texts, prophets have that gift; however, we can have it too, so that it could help us to take control of our life. This is what is stated at Genesis (41: 25-35)

25. Then Joseph said to Pharaoh, "The dreams of Pharaoh are one and the same. God has revealed to Pharaoh what he is about to do.

26. The seven good cows are seven years, and the seven good heads of grain are seven years; it is one and the same dream.

27. The seven lean, ugly cows that came up afterward are seven years, and so are the seven worthless heads of grain scorched by the east wind: They are seven years of famine.

28. "It is just as I said to Pharaoh: God has shown Pharaoh what he is about to do.

29. Seven years of great abundance are coming throughout the land of Egypt,

30. But seven years of famine will follow them. Then all the abundance in Egypt will be forgotten, and the famine will ravage the land.

31. The abundance in the land will not be remembered, because the famine that follows it will be so severe.

32. The reason the dream was given to Pharaoh in two forms is that the matter has been firmly decided by God, and God will do it soon.

After this revelation, the Pharaoh appointed Joseph on top of all Egypt, so that he would be the prime minister and manage all his lands and belongings.

The Gift of Acknowledgement John (5:39-44).

> *39. You study the Scriptures diligently because you think that in them you have eternal life. These are the very Scriptures that testify about me,*
>
> *40. yet you refuse to come to me to have life.*
>
> *41. "I do not accept glory from human beings,*
>
> *42. but I know you. I know that you do not have the love of God in your hearts.*
>
> *43. I have come in my Father's name, and you do not accept me; but if someone else comes in his own name, you will accept him.*
>
> *44. How can you believe since you accept glory from one another but do not seek the glory that comes from the only God?*

We have to acknowledge and accept that we are children of God and thank Him for the gifts that we have received through the Holy Spirit, being certain that the gifts that we have received are for honor and glory of the Lord and its people. Just as we thank others that help us or serve us, likewise, we must thank God for what we are and have.

Definitely, God has placed gifts and talents in you, so that you can make them work on the benefit of others and yourself, always for the honor and glory of the Lord.

In order to do that, you have to know yourself. Seek inside and discover your passion. Discover those things that you love and enjoy, those that you always do right when you do

them. Those things that require almost no effort from you, but that you always do right, or, even when they do require an effort from your side, it is always a satisfying effort.

They are those things that you do voluntarily, without anyone asking you to do so. It is when your skills, your passion and your personal attitude are at the same level, comprising a key point for the combination of your gifts and talents. Therefore, it is important to consider that talent and passion are side by side. What you want to discover is what truly fills you with joy and what you would do even if you don't get paid for it.

Ask yourself, who are you, what are your gifts and talents, what are those things that you love to do and where your talent stands out, what is that thing that takes your sleep away every time you are thinking and working about something. How can you make a difference with the gifts and talents that God has given you? What product or service can you give others through your gifts?

The Gift of Service:

Everyone that has the gift of service is dedicated to helping others and does it with an open and full of love heart, with a positive attitude that attracts others, creating around it an environment of harmony and safety for those that receive it. These persons have the capacity of discovering the needs of others and giving them a hand, without taking into consideration the discomfort it may cause on themselves doing so. They are capable of walking the extra mile, just to help and serve others. Their service has a unique characteristic; those receiving it feel blessed and fortunate for receiving such support.

If we used our gifts and talents, we would open new windows of opportunities for growing in the world that we are living, as we expand our knowledge and relationships with others. If your strength is helping, dedicate yourself to the service of others. Your gifts and talents will open opportunities for you to reach and help more people that are lacking your knowledge, products or services. You'll be able to reach the people in need in a positive way and help lots of them. If you dedicate yourself to serving and helping others, God will reward you for your effort and sacrifice, by one hundred times by one. It is as the planter who with only one corn seed obtains an abundant harvest.

For helping and serving you need effort, sacrifice, time and money. It is a Price that not everyone is willing to pay, but for those that do, they find themselves well rewarded for their job. They think about how things can be, not about how they are; they see a world of possibilities and new opportunities for all. It is adding and multiplying instead of dividing and subtracting. It is leaving your comfort zone only to bring value to others.

If you like to help and serve, ask yourself the following questions: What are my gifts and talents? How can I be useful with the gifts that I possess? What services or products can I provide to others? How can I make a difference for others? Think about all the options there are and the traits that you possess for making a difference.

Help or Support

It is giving support to the one in need, directly or indirectly, by offering our time and personal resources. It is giving a hand or helping other without expecting anything in return.

It consists of giving without receiving in order to make this world a better place. It is looking at the needs of others and contributing to the cause. Serving is a way of thanking God for everything that He has given us, for the health, the family, the job and/or the business, for the gift of wisdom, the understanding, and because He guides our steps through the path of goodness, so that today we can enjoy the blessings that we are receiving through his grace.

There are different ways of showing the gift of service. It can be through a contribution of our time or of any knowledge that we have. Another way of contributing is through our gifts and talents, by making decisions to change our fate and the fate of others through the creation of jobs and products. Nowadays we have lots of companies that have offered their articles and services, changing our way of living and our quality of life for several generations.

It is important to acknowledge the power of our thoughts. When what we think connects with our gifts and talents, a world of possibilities arises, capable of changing the fate of one person as well of a full nation. For example, today we can see as technology and science has revolutionized the world, creating new and better opportunities for everyone.

Probably, you will find yourself working today for a company that isn't yours, which is providing you with livelihood. These companies have been there, in the market, for many years, offering jobs and services to everyone in need.

All these companies, without exemption, have arisen from a thought that came alive at each of its founders, and have revolutionized the world that we live on. You can also change your destiny by helping others. God has given you talents and gifts, and only you can use them, but it is your duty to

discover them, thus creating a better world full of opportunities for everyone.

The business world has a way of contributing that can even cause an impact on personal, spiritual and economical. As we can see, there are lots of ways in which you can contribute something to anyone in need, only by being willing to do so. Seek inside yourself and discover the being living inside you, deep inside you, and discover your gifts and talents so that you can also do your part, by helping others. Dedicate yourself to growing and being the best version of you. Become that, what you were created for. Even your example can be a light of hope for others and a way of contributing.

Dare and expand your view towards the almighty, our Creator, and don't let fear stop you, as you can be the difference. If you are reading this book it is because you have faith and you see a light at the end of the tunnel. But you have to chase what is calling you and has your name on it, that thing that is saying "come and find me". I assure you that you will get to places that you never imagined before and you will reach dreams that are unreachable for many, but you will accomplish.

Your gifts are calling you and your dreams await you.

Ask yourself the following questions: What can I do to change my destiny and my family's? How can I make a difference on the life of others? What gifts and talents do I possess that could enable me to help others? What do I enjoy doing and that when I do it, I feel very good? Can I see an opportunity of offering my time or my services on that which I enjoy doing?

When we use our gifts and talents and we put them to the service of others, we help to make this world a better place with new possibilities and new opportunities.

- **What are those things that upset you?**

When you discover yourself, not only will you discover everything that matters to you, but you will also find those things that make you feel bad or that you don't like when they happen. Here is an opportunity for you to find out the part of you that makes you feel vulnerable, so that you can work it out and overcome it.

What are those things that when they happen they upset you? Those things that make feel bad? The things you would change if you could? They could be behaviors, attitudes or actions that affect us spiritually, physically, emotionally, at our family or economy. Is this an opportunity for yourself to change and at the same time help others to change? Can you find an opportunity for you to offer a product or service to the one in need?

- **Know your weaknesses**

Knowing your virtues and traits, gifts and talents is important as it helps you to accomplish your purpose, but acknowledging your weaknesses is far more important, as they are what keeps you paralyzed or stops you from moving on. You have to acknowledge it, so that you can overcome it. Your weaknesses are those negative characteristics that restrain you from growing. It is your negative way of thinking and acting what is stopping you. Think about all that is stopping you from being the vest version of yourself.

CHAPTER 2: DISCOVER YOUR DREAMS, PROJECTS, AND PRIORITIES:

"Once you have discovered something to die for, you would have found a reason to live".

(Anonymous)

Why is it important to know what we want?

To know what we want helps us focusing on the things that matter in our life. It means going after what makes us happy and passionate. When we know what we want, we feel fulfilled, because every step and movement we make is towards the thing that we want and makes us feel connected to the being living inside us.

To know what we want helps us to be more productive, we work faster, better and with more efficiency. It helps us to save time and money as we can focus on the things that we really care about, instead of finding alternatives that wouldn't really add any value into our life.

Get a moment of the time that God has given you and ask yourself: What do I really want for my life? What is my purpose in life? What was I created for? Search deep within yourself and discover your purpose, so that you don't have to spend your life wondering what you truly want and doing something that you were not created for.

Your Dreams

Dreams are a result of our thoughts and wishes in the pursuit for happiness. Those are the ideas that fill us with satisfaction and happiness when thinking about them.

Dreams give our existence meaning. They provide a reason to be, feel and live. When dreams are really our own, God and the universe conspire in our favor, so that we can make them true, through events and situations.

That is why we need to listen to our internal voice, because deep within ourselves there is a silent, simple, and honest voice, it's like the child living in us, it is called **life's purpose.**

When you discover your life's purpose, the search for your dreams and for that thing that would supposedly make you happy will come to an end, as you would have found the thing that you were created for. Therefore, it is very important to look inside yourself and ask: Who am I? What is my purpose in life? How can I discover my purpose? What are my dreams? What do I really want to accomplish in life? Why are my dreams important to me? And how can I fulfill them?

By doing this exercise, your objective will be to discover yourself, search deep within your being, to know who you really are, so that you can find the truth inside you.

Your Goals

Goals are planning for fulfilling our dreams. It is the process that we are going to develop in order to achieve those things that are fundamental to us. To establish goals gives our life meaning and purpose and, when we achieve them, we are applying one way to make our dreams come true. By reaching these goals we get a feeling of progress and success that helps us to be happier.

To achieve our goals, whether it is on the short or the long term, gives us trust and helps us to believe in ourselves. Short-term goals could be a day, a week, a month or even a year,

while long-term goals could be from two to three years, five, ten or even twenty or more.

Short-Term Goals

Short-term goals could seem like they are of very small interest or importance at all; however, the reality is that they play a decisive role as they make us feel good when we achieve them, at the same time, they drive us one step closer to the fulfillment of our dreams. Short-term goals are like seeing a child take his first steps; it is an achievement that fills us with joy, as we can see the child growing strong. The same thing happens when we achieve our short-term goals, as we feel that we are moving forward day by day, in the fulfillment of our objectives.

People who achieve daily goals tend to feel happier and more optimistic than those who don't have any goals. By being optimistic, they can endure the adversities during hard times. Unfortunately, most of us have the natural tendency of being pessimistic, of seeing the cup half empty and putting difficulties first. As a result, undertaking daily goals or short term goals makes us feel useful at the same time that we are realizing that we are moving forward.

Long-Term Goals

They usually cover a project that could last for several years before being undertaken.

They are about a project where many factors play a critical role for the accomplishment of dreams. Long-term goals require lots of courage, character, attitude, effort, sacrifice, and most of all, lots of faith, actions, discipline and persistence. When we are able to reunite and develop those

qualities, we plant the seeds of **abundance** in us, and those seeds will be passed from this generation to the generations to come for living many long years.

When we set goals, whether they are on the short or the long term, we also have to set a timeframe for achieving them. We cannot leave our objectives to luck, or without setting a specific date. Otherwise, the risk will be that the objective may never be met.

When we define a timeframe. It has to be reasonable, unhurriedly and with considerations. Even if you wish to see changes and results quickly, and you want everything to be carried out immediately, it usually won't turn out to be that way. It will all be part of a process and will take time. Therefore, it is very important to have a long-term vision and, in it we must take into consideration some of the following details:

1) Knowing what you want to achieve.

2) Knowing why is that thing you want important for you

3) Knowing how you are going to achieve it.

4) Knowing when do you want to achieve it.

5) Taking action, until achieving your objective.

If you take all these five steps into consideration, and you act on them on a daily basis, you won't have to worry for anything else, because time and results will speak for themselves.

When you set out into achieving a goal and you believe you can achieve it in two or three (2-3) years, take at least five or six (5-6) years to do so; as in the process you will find events and situations out of your control, which are not part of your

plans. It is good to consider the steps that you need to follow in order to achieve it. You must be realistic and patient with the time that it will take, as, if you establish a rushed or impossible goal, the only thing that you will get is frustration, by thinking that all you did is was a failure and a waste of time, when in reality all that was missing was patience and time to get to the goal.

Set Your Priorities in Order

Priorities give our life direction. Through them we recognize what are the most critical things for us, among all the things that we deem important. It means putting first the things with a unique value for us, those that need the most attention possible, so that we can schedule and use our time, in combination with the necessary energy, towards the right purposes.

People who don't set priorities are exposed to taking paths that are not suited for their needs. They spend most of their time in matters of minor importance, or even worse, on activities that have nothing to do with their objectives.

But, if you are able to define your priorities, you will find the right path towards your priority and your reality, in such a way that you will invest your time efficiently in order to achieve your objectives.

Having an objective is easy; to achieve it is harder. When we talk about priorities, we talk about things that matter to us, from those things that require effort and sacrifice, based mainly on action, discipline and persistence. It is beginning immediately and looking towards tomorrow, as only continuous and well carried out job will deliver the desired outcomes.

We all wish to have good physical, spiritual, emotional/mental, familiar, and economical health.

Even if I acknowledge that we all have different dreams and projects, at the end, our dreams and projects will end up within one or maybe all five of these priorities.

Therefore, it is important to arrange them in order of priority; this will help us to focus our time and energy in an efficient way.

Spiritual Health

We all wish to have good emotional, physical, familiar, and economical health. However, even if these priorities are crucial for the human being, it is also fundamental to give spiritual peace a great importance. It is no good for us to have health, love, and money if we don't have peace inside us. We've heard of very famous people that may have had all in life, from physical and familiar love, to fame and money, along with all the luxuries that life could offer; but that have chosen to end their lives and are not here with us anymore, as they didn't feel at peace with God or with themselves.

Others have chosen to abandon themselves in the world of drugs and alcohol, whether due to their own decision or because they didn't know how to deal with money and fame. Also, there are some that have been desperate about money and the lack of it or just because they haven't handled properly the situations and problems that overwhelm them.

Instead, when we are people of **faith** and we have spiritual health, we are not only at peace with ourselves but also with God and with the others. This doesn't mean that we would be free of trouble, but God will give us the wisdom needed so that we can distinguish before life's adversities and find a

solution for the situations torturing us without having to use drugs or alcohol, or even worse, to go against our own life or the life of others.

Mental and Physical Health

When we talk about health, not only do we talk about physical health, but also about mental health. A good mental health can be described as the condition in which both our body and mind are functioning properly.

Keeping a good physical and mental health allows us to undertake the physical activities that we enjoy due to the fact that we are at the right conditions: activities like going out for dinner or dancing, exercising, walking in the park, going to the beach, enjoying some nice vacations, without having any disability that could affect us or that we couldn't handle. It's being able to enjoy all physical and mental activities that you feel attracted for only because you are in good health.

Also, enjoying good health allows us to fulfill our daily responsibilities and take care of the things that matter to us. This way we can fulfill our home and work obligations. Enjoying good health allows us to take care of our families without having any obstacle or being able to attend the circumstances that appear. You only depend on yourself for choosing and executing decisions that matter in your life without having to depend on anyone else.

Mental/Emotional Health

Emotional health is based on feeling good with ourselves. Feeling good emotionally allows us to improve our physical health. The positive state of mind of a person improves health

and prevents the risk of getting sick, as well as reduces the risk of getting depression and anxiety.

When we find ourselves at a good emotional state, we relate better to others and we are capable of controlling our thoughts and feelings, as well as our decisions and actions. We have the capability of controlling emotions in a natural way, for facing daily problems without having to live all stressed because of them.

We must recognize that spiritual, physical and emotional health are three priorities that are very important in our lives, because they all have to do with events and situations that happen to us internally, while familiar and economic priorities are events and situations happening externally, even if they affect us directly.

These three priorities are the fundamental base of the human being, as they are the starting point of each success or failure for the individual. Thus, maintaining a good spiritual, physical and emotional state plays a key role in every life, as the personal, familiar, and economic development depends on it.

Family

Maintaining a bearable relationship with our family is achieved through having good communication with all its members. Good communication allows to spend more time with the loved ones and to achieve a daily harmonious development on the living activities between them.

An effective communication at the family group results in living in a happy and responsible home. Its members are capable of working out their differences in a good way, as the main priority is the family and not their personal interests.

This way, a feeling of emotional stability is abided on all home members.

Finances

Finances play a very important role in our lives, as they help us to pay for basic needs as well as to satisfy other essential needs in our daily living. In order to maintain a better life quality and to increase the economic development of the individual, it is required to handle finances carefully.

Enjoying good economic health allows us to choose the quality of life that we want to achieve and not the one that we are forced to live due to the lack of it. It is being economically free to choose where do you want to live, the school that your children will attend to, the car we want to drive, when and where will our next vacation be, not having to be worried about where we will get the money from. Having good economy allows you to design your own life, instead of just living it without a choice.

Economic stability also allows us to contribute to the social and economic development of the country or city that we live in. This can be achieved through the contributions originated from the payment of taxes for the creation of hospitals, schools, bridges, and highways, among others. It is also helpful for creating companies and improving our quality-of-life through available products and services, at the time that job sources are originated for those in need of jobs.

These five priorities work as the human body. Your body is comprised from different organs and each one of them carries out a specific function, but they are all part of the same body. If an organ stops working, the body results affected, as it doesn't work the same, because that specific organ carries

out a function that is inter-dependent with others inside the body.

The same goes for these five priorities. Even if each one of them plays a different role, they are all part of the same set of priorities. If one of them turns out to be affected, all other priorities will also be affected as they are part of the same body of priorities that are integrated within our life.

We must take care of them, as they all intervene to have a healthy spiritual, physical, emotional, familiar, and economical life.

CHAPTER 3
YOUR SPIRITUAL LIFE

Why is it important to follow a Spiritual Life?

Living under the grace of God helps us to live a life of internal harmony and peace, a life full of hope and possibilities, a more balanced life, not only regarding spiritual but also emotional matters, all of which helps us to achieve a pleasant level of joy and happiness.

The five priorities exposed in the paragraphs above are the ones that are the most relevant, but among all of them, the one we highlight is spiritual, as it is the fundamental basis upon which all others are built. It is this way, because your life will depend on the harmonious relationship that you have with yourself and our Creator, which means that you have to value more internal and spiritual matters than external or material ones.

In order for us to fully function and reach our maximum potential, by generating a high performance, we have to be at spiritual harmony. This way we would be able to enjoy a good physical, emotional, familiar, and economical life, keeping a good balance between those priorities.

Seeking from God with a True Heart

Regarding that necessary balance, Matthew 7: 7-11 talks about praying as the golden rule:

> 7. *"Ask and it will be given to you; seek and you will find; knock and the door will be opened to you.*

> *8. For everyone who asks receives; the one who seeks finds; and to the one who knocks, the door will be opened.*
>
> *9. "Which of you, if your son asks for bread, will give him a stone?*
>
> *10. Or if he asks for a fish, will give him a snake?*
>
> *11. If you, then, though you are evil, know how to give good gifts to your children, how much more will your Father in heaven give good gifts to those who ask him*

Understanding that we are children of God and that the Lord wants whatever is best for us, helps us to trust in Him more, just as a child who puts all his trust in his father. Likewise, we must trust the Lord and ask him for his help and guidance, so that we can achieve our objectives. But we must ask Him with an unbreakable faith, as for Him, nothing is impossible.

He also invites us out of our comfort zone and to take the actions required in order to achieve our objectives, because those who seek will find, and the door will be opened to the one that knocks.

Our role in front of others

Along with praying, Matthew 5: 14-16 also presents us with a very valuable element:

> *14. "You are the light of the world. A town built on a hill cannot be hidden.*

> *14. "You are the light of the world. A town built on a hill cannot be hidden.*
>
> *15. Neither do people light a lamp and put it under a bowl. Instead, they put it on its stand, and it gives light to everyone in the house*
>
> *16. In the same way, let your light shine before others, that they may see your good deeds and glorify your Father in heaven.*

God wants us to be light and hope for others, both at the spiritual and the personal. Let we broaden our sight towards the Lord, so that He can pour His blessings over all of us and so that these blessings serve as an example for others, while being honor and glory for the Creator. Let our thoughts, labor and actions be a light of hope for those in need.

When you go to sleep at night, place your shoes under your bed, as far as possible, so that when you wake up in the morning, you'll have to kneel in order to reach them. While kneeling ask the Lord for help, but also, let yourself be shaped, just as the mud is shaped when soft, so that He would do his work of art out of you. Ask him to help you discover the gifts and talents He has placed in you, so that you could help others to do the same thing, and so that, through these gifts you could reach places so high that you would never have imagined before, remembering, always, to keep love and humbleness first, so that you could live a successful life, full of abundance, without becoming an arrogant, pushy, proud or haughty person.

In all that we are explaining we cannot deny our human condition, in which we also include our weaknesses, but this something that we have to handle by counting on God's guidance. We just have to take a look at the Gospel of John (20 : 24-25) about the doubt as a characteristic and weakness for any person:

Happy are those who have a Humble Heart

We are going to take a moment and stop at Matthew 13: 10-17 to think about ourselves and some of our own experiences:

> *The purpose of Parables*
>
> *10. The disciples came to him and asked, "Why do you speak to the people in parables?"*
>
> *11. He replied, "Because the knowledge of the secrets of the kingdom of heaven has been given to you, but not to them.*
>
> *12. Whoever has will be given more, and they will have an abundance. Whoever does not have, even what they have will be taken from them.*
>
> *13. This is why I speak to them in parables: "Though seeing, they do not see though hearing, they do not hear or understand.*
>
> *14. In them is fulfilled the prophecy of Isaiah:" 'You will be ever hearing but never understanding; you will be ever seeing but never perceiving.*
>
> *15. For this people's heart has become calloused; they hardly hear with their ears, and they have closed their eyes. Otherwise they might see with their eyes, hear with their ears, understand with their hearts and turn, and I would heal them.'*

> *16. But blessed are your eyes because they see, and your ears because they hear.*
>
> *17. For truly I tell you, many prophets and righteous people longed to see what you see but did not see it, and to hear what you hear but did not hear it.*

This happens to a lot of us, that don't listen, and if we do listen, we don't understand. If we understand, we don't act accordingly with God's will, or with the principles of success and the natural laws.

How many times have we lied or slandered innocent people, only to look good in front of others? How many times have we been more worried about what others think about us, than about what God and you think about yourself? How many times have we left the things that we have to do in order to improve our quality of life undone, only due to the fear of the unknown or fear of failure? How many times have you chosen to hear a lie that makes you happy at the moment, instead of the truth that shall set you free? How many times have we denied saying yes to the opportunities that God offers, only because of failure, thus denying us a greater wellness? How many times have we sacrificed our children to a life of plenty needs and absences due to a lack of effort and sacrifice, depriving them of the opportunity of living a healthy life and full of possibilities?

For how long will we continue like this, denying the grace that God has kept for us, due to the fear of failure or fear of what people may say?

We are going to ask the Lord for the gift of wisdom, so that we can distinguish between good and evil, fare and unfair, right, and wrong.

For him to give us the gift of knowledge and intelligence so that we can watch when we look, understand when we listen and accept things even if we don't understand them, so that we can act accordingly with what is expected from us.

For him to give us the gift of acknowledgment, so that we can see the opportunities that we have through the gifts that we have received, as only then will we be able to achieve the desired objectives through the Holy Spirit, for the honor and glory of the Lord.

The words of Matthew (5:3) outline humbleness as an attitude that goes along with praying:

> *3. Blessed are the poor in spirit, for theirs is the kingdom of heaven.*

Blessed are the humble in heart, as God will give them knowledge and understanding so that they can handle adversities. Blessed are the humble, as they will know the necessities of others and therefore, will be able to make the world we live in, a better place. Blessed are the humble in heart, as they seek the Lord at all times, and make Him part of their lives. Blessed are the humble, as in the moments of harvest, He will fill them with abundance and prosperity so that they can keep on blessing others. Blessed are the humble, as, in their moments of difficulty the Lord will make them strong with His Spirit and will give them the wisdom needed to fight the battles.

Patience and Trust

A very timely observation for the days that we are currently living is stated at Matthew (5:5):

> 5. Blessed are the meek, for they will inherit the earth.

Because the ones that know how to wait can understand God's plan and recognize that God's timing is always perfect. The thing that you are wishing for will not arrive a minute or a second too late. The one that knows how to be patient understands that everything is a process and in this process, God is doing his perfect work out of him and out of everyone. Mothers acknowledge the importance of time. They know how to wait patiently during the nine months of pregnancy, so that they can later give birth to the beautiful baby that has carried in her wound. Even if they feel anxious to have that baby in their arms, they wait all that time because they wish for a healthy child.

Patience brings along the fruits and blessings that God has kept for us, but we have to understand that God's timing is perfect and He is never wrong. Ask God for the gift of understanding and patience so that you can accept his mysteries. Remember that you wouldn't achieve your objectives based on your own strength, but only through the Holy Spirit, as He acts over you in mysterious ways.

Keep an Unbreakable Faith. John (20: 24-25)

> *24. Now Thomas (also known as Didymus[a]), one of the Twelve, was not with the disciples when Jesus came.*
>
> *25. So the other disciples told him, "We have seen the Lord! "But he said to them, "Unless I see the nail marks in his hands and put my finger where the nails were, and put my hand into his side, I will not believe.".*

Jesus tells us about not being unbelievers and about trusting in Him more, about putting all our trust in Him through faith, about us keeping our faith in place, even at the most difficult times of our life. Because faith is the only thing that leads us to action when the invisible is still not visible, because everything is possible through faith

John (20: 26-29) continues the story and lets us know what Jesus is trying to teach:

> *26. A week later his disciples were in the house again and Thomas was with them. Though the doors were locked, Jesus came and stood among them and said, "Peace be with you!"*
>
> *27. Then he said to Thomas, "Put your finger here; see my hands. Reach out your hand and put it into my side. Stop doubting and believe.".*
>
> *28. Thomas said to him, "My Lord and my God!"*
>
> *29. Then Jesus told him, "Because you have seen me, you have believed; blessed are those who have not seen and yet have believed."*

I don't know what your situation is or what are your objectives, but I am sure of one thing: we need to trust something or someone, and, who better than God, our Creator, the One who gave away his only son for us. Then, why shouldn't we trust him? Seek for him with faith and don't be like Thomas, that only believed because he saw. You are blessed if you believe before seeing, as only then will you see through faith.

The faith we are talking about is outlined in Matthew (8: 5-8):

> *The Faith of the Centurion*
>
> *5. When Jesus had entered Capernaum, a centurion came to him, asking for help.*
>
> *6. "Lord," he said, "my servant lies at home paralyzed, suffering terribly."*
>
> *7. Jesus said to him, "Shall I come and heal him?"*
>
> *8. The centurion replied, "Lord, I do not deserve to have you come under my roof. But just say the word, and my servant will be healed.*

Jesus felt surprised about how big the faith on the centurion's answer was. The centurion acknowledged the power that Jesus had for healing his servant, and that is why he deposited all his trust in Him, to the point that he went begging for Him to heal his servant. By having such a strong faith, he knew that Jesus had to do nothing in order to heal the servant, and that he would do it only by saying the word.

This is the faith we should all have in the Lord, so that He can work on each and every one of us. That is why I am telling you again, I don't know what your situation is, or what are your plans and projects and objectives in life, but I can assure you one thing: it won't be through your own strength that you will achieve it, but through the Holy Spirit.

The Centurion's story keeps unfolding in Matthew (8 : 9-13), to show us faith even further:

> *9. For I myself am a man under authority, with soldiers under me. I tell this one, 'Go,' and he goes; and that one, 'Come,' and he comes. I say to my servant, 'Do this,' and he does it."*
>
> *10. When Jesus heard this, he was amazed and said to those following him, "Truly I tell you, I have not found anyone in Israel with such great faith.*
>
> *11. I say to you that many will come from the east and the west, and will take their places at the feast with Abraham, Isaac and Jacob in the kingdom of heaven.*
>
> *12. But the subjects of the kingdom will be thrown outside, into the darkness, where there will be weeping and gnashing of teeth."*
>
> *13. Then Jesus said to the centurion, "Go! Let it be done just as you believed it would." And his servant was healed at that moment.*

God, our Lord, acts in mysterious ways, and we will never understand his plans, but if we want to reach our full potential and achieve our objectives, we only have to deposit our entire trust in Him through **faith,** so that his actions could manifest on us.

Discover and Develop your Talents

Side by side with faith, we find the compassionate feelings, as explained in Matthew (9: 35-38)

> *The Workers Are Few*
>
> *35. Jesus went through all the towns and villages, teaching in their synagogues, proclaiming the good news of the kingdom and healing every disease and sickness.*
>
> *36. When he saw the crowds, he had compassion on them, because they were harassed and helpless, like sheep without a shepherd.*
>
> *37. Then he said to his disciples, "The harvest is plentiful but the workers are few.*
>
> *38. Ask the Lord of the harvest, therefore, to send out workers into his harvest field."*

God has placed in you gifts and talents and only you can put them into good use; He wants you to discover them and put them to work for the benefit of others and for the honor and glory of the Lord. He wants us to give our best, always, and to be a light of hope for others, because the harvest is abundant but the workers are few, carrying the good news to everyone who needs it through the already received gifts and talents. Because only by helping others, you will help yourself.

God wants us to be the best we can be, according to his commands, and that our actions be an example for others and for generations to come. And that we plant good seeds with the gifts that we have received so that our harvest will always be rich.

Discover your gifts, discover your talents and put them to work for the service of others so that they can take you to places that you have never imagined before. Harvest your ideas with a different vision, also considering the possibilities and not only what it is. Don't be afraid and look at the opportunities that God has for you because the harvest is abundant, but the workers are few.

How do we embrace Lord's lessons?

We often listen "Every person is a whole world to explore". Even if we sometimes live similar experiences or receive the same instructions, usually persons react differently. The different attitudes of the human being are described in Matthew (25:14-30):

> *The Parable of the Bags of Gold*
>
> *14. "Again, it will be like a man going on a journey, who called his servants and entrusted his wealth to them.*
>
> *15. To one he gave five bags of gold, to another two bags, and to another one bag,[a] each according to his ability. Then he went on his journey.*
>
> *16. The man who had received five bags of gold went at once and put his money to work and gained five bags more.*
>
> *17. So also, the one with two bags of gold gained two more.*
>
> *18. But the man who had received one bag went off, dug a hole in the ground and hid his master's money.*
>
> *19. "After a long time the master of those servants returned and settled accounts with them.*

20. The man who had received five bags of gold brought the other five. 'Master,' he said, 'you entrusted me with five bags of gold. See, I have gained five more.'

21. "His master replied, 'Well done, good and faithful servant! You have been faithful with a few things; I will put you in charge of many things. Come and share your master's happiness!'

22. "The man with two bags of gold also came. 'Master,' he said, 'you entrusted me with two bags of gold; see, I have gained two more.'

23. "His master replied, 'Well done, good and faithful servant! You have been faithful with a few things; I will put you in charge of many things. Come and share your master's happiness!'

24. "Then the man who had received one bag of gold came. 'Master,' he said, 'I knew that you are a hard man, harvesting where you have not sown and gathering where you have not scattered seed.

25. ere is what belongs to you.

26. "His master replied, 'You wicked, lazy servant! So you knew that I harvest where I have not sown and gather where I have not scattered seed?

27. Well then, you should have put my money on deposit with the bankers, so that when I returned I would have received it back with interest.

28. 'So take the bag of gold from him and give it to the one who has ten bags.

> *29. For whoever has will be given more, and they will have an abundance. Whoever does not have, even what they have will be taken from them.*
>
> *30. And throw that worthless servant outside, into the darkness, where there will be weeping and gnashing of teeth.'*

God wishes for us to be prosperous and to live a life of abundance, which is why He has placed in each and every one of us gifts and talents, so that we can put them into practice for the service of others. He wants us to be successful, and that, through our gifts, we could become a light of hope for others, without becoming arrogant, pushy or pride, because the more we grow the greater the honor and glory of the Lord. But remember, if you don't use your talents, you will be a slave of those who do, and your talents will be stripped from you or will die with you, as you never gave them life.

Wisdom

The lord has given us wisdom because He wishes for us to learn all that we can about heaven, earth and everything regarding his work, within our reach, because this way we can reach a spiritual and mental capacity that would help us to make better decisions for a life lived in prosperity and holiness. Therefore, it is important to gain knowledge studying as a means for receiving the blessings that the Lord has for us, not forgetting to thank Him. Otherwise, we will get lost in the way and never arrive to the truth. This is mentioned in several sentences of Wisdom (3 : 7-12)

> *7. In the time of their visitation they will shine forth, and will run like sparks through the stubble.*
>
> *8. They will govern nations and rule over peoples, and the Lord will reign over them forever.*
>
> *9. Those who trust in him will understand truth, and the faithful will abide with him in love,*
>
> *10. But the ungodly will be punished as their reasoning deserves, those who disregarded the righteous*
>
> *and rebelled against the Lord;*
>
> *11. for those who despise wisdom and instruction are miserable. Their hope is vain, their labors are unprofitable, and their works are useless.*
>
> *12. Their wives are foolish, and their children evil; their offspring are accursed.*

The Lord wishes that we try hard to learn and grow, because the one who doesn't learn cannot grow. The one who doesn't learn doesn't grow, and the one who doesn't grow lives a life, his own life; a life full of limitations and absence due to the lack of information and knowledge. "For them every hope is vain, every effort is useless, and every work is infertile. Also, his wife and children will suffer the consequences of his acts, because you cannot give what you don't have and you cannot teach what you don't know.

The Storm

Even after all the time that has passed since those days, Matthew (8:23-27) describes similar situations to the ones that we may be going through now, and that make us forget about patience and trust in the expectation of the Lord:

> *Jesus Calms the Storm*
>
> *23. Then he got into the boat and his disciples followed him.*
>
> *24. Suddenly a furious storm came up on the lake, so that the waves swept over the boat. But Jesus was sleeping.*
>
> *25. The disciples went and woke him, saying, "Lord, save us! We're going to drown!"*
>
> *26. He replied, "You of little faith, why are you so afraid?" Then he got up and rebuked the winds and the waves, and it was completely calm.*
>
> *27. The men were amazed and asked, "What kind of man is this? Even the winds and the waves obey him!"*

Jesus lets us know that hard times will come, dark and stormy times. Therefore, troubles will test our faith, will make us doubt about our belief in the Lord, to the point that we would even doubt if God exists. Many times, we will be convinced that there are no possibilities to get out of all the problems haunting us.

But, if we support ourselves in the Lord, He will give us the required strength for moving forward. He will give us wisdom and understanding to face situations. He will guide us through the right path when facing our adversities and

fighting our battles. This means that, if we trust the Lord, we shouldn't feel afraid or be worried as He is in control. Worries are a sign that we don't trust Him, and that we will act by our own will. By doing so, we will be acting alone and without the grace of God.

Blessings and Obligations

There are matters that we have to attend in our daily life, as members of a society, though these responsibilities don't mean to leave God aside. The reading at Mark (12 : 13-17) is direct and clear when dealing with this matter:

> *Paying the Imperial Tax to Caesar*
>
> *13. Later they sent some of the Pharisees and Herodians to Jesus to catch him in his words.*
>
> *14. They came to him and said, "Teacher, we know that you are a man of integrity. You aren't swayed by others, because you pay no attention to who they are; but you teach the way of God in accordance with the truth. Is it right to pay the imperial tax to Caesar or not?*
>
> *15. Should we pay or shouldn't we? "But Jesus knew their hypocrisy. "Why are you trying to trap me?" he asked. "Bring me a denarius and let me look at it."*
>
> *16. They brought the coin, and he asked them, "Whose image is this? And whose inscription?" "Caesar's," they replied.*
>
> *17. Then Jesus said to them, "Give back to Caesar what is Caesar's and to God what is God's." And they were amazed at him.*

The Lord wants us to be responsible with our obligations and finances.

"Give to Caesar what belongs to Caesar", means paying our taxes and complying with the financial obligations we have with others. Paying taxes is a duty for building schools and hospitals, bridges, and roads, as well as other essential services in the city or country that we live on.

Likewise, "Give to God what belongs to God" (the tithe, 10%), means the charity work that we are doing for our fellow man through the tithe, at the time we follow his commands. Why should we contribute like this?

Through the tithe, the Lord fills us with many blessings because He recognizes our good intentions with our neighbors, which makes us deserve much more, so that we can continue helping others.

Firstly, the Lord will continue to give you the intelligence and wisdom needed so that you can continue to make good decisions with the ninety percent (90%) of your remaining goods. He will make sure that you learn how to handle your finances correctly, so that you will be able to cover for all your needs, and also, that multiply your investment.

He will not only protect you from those trying to harm you or your loved ones, but he will also put persons, situations, and events on your way, so that you will come out triumphant and keep blessing those that are most needed.

The Lord is a fare Father to all of us. But those who don't share with the fellow man the blessings that God has given them, will always live-in need, and not even one hundred percent (100%) of their income/goods will be enough for them to cover their personal needs.

If you can't contribute with the tithe, because you have other commitments, then begin by giving a minor percentage, but remember God will bless you accordingly to your intentions and your deeds of charity. Careful here, as it is not giving only because you feel obliged to, or because you want to get something in return; because God doesn't like when you do anything out of obligation, but instead when you do out of love for Him and others. Remember that He knows your thoughts and also your intentions.

Remember, helping the one in need and carrying out charity deeds is a way of gratitude, it is thanking God for giving us life, job and business, our family, our understanding, and wisdom to make good decisions at every moment. It is showing our gratitude to the fact that He takes care of us and of our loved ones, as well as of our finances. It is transmitting gratitude towards Him, for all his blessings. It is saying to Him "thank you Lord, as you are in control, enlightening my steps and my destiny".

I invite you to do these three things every day in the morning; but you must do them with an open heart and with love:

1: Widen your mind towards the Lord; so that He fills it with wisdom.

2: Open your heart and He will fill it with love, peace and humbleness

3: Spread your hands and the Lord shall fill them with abundance.

CHAPTER 4
PHYSICAL, EMOTIONAL AND MENTAL HEALTH

Your Physical Health

Taking control of our health is as important as taking control of our finances. Having health issues will not only affect us physically but also emotionally and mentally. Therefore, keeping good health must be a priority in our life.

I know that all of us, at some point in our lives, have had, are having or will have some disease, but it is important to undertake physical activities, in order to contribute to a basic state of good mental and physical health. Physical activities can be more beneficial than we think, as they are not only good for losing weight but also to keep us in good shape.

Undertaking physical activities means moving your body or keeping it active for burning calories and stimulating your metabolism. That is why, activities like walking, running, riding a bicycle, aerobics or playing a sport, are recommended, as well as any body movement that would require spending energy. Something that we must point out is that these physical activities should be moderated and constant, in order to be able to obtain really beneficial effects on our health and on the prevention of diseases.

There are different benefits of physical activity. Usually, it helps to relief stress, as it is a natural way of fighting and reducing symptoms of anxiety and depression, and it also reduces blood pressure and the risk of getting diabetes and cardiovascular diseases. It is a way to prevent muscular

diseases and osteoporosis. It helps us to control our weight when burning calories.

Those who live a physically more active life, often live longer than those who live a sedentary life or with less activity. This means that activities can be the prescribed antidote for improving our physical, emotional and mental health, as they can not only help us with physical wellbeing but also to increase our self-esteem because they make us look and feel better.

Your Emotional Health

Enjoying good physical health is one of our life's priorities, but when we also have mental and emotional health, our life changes completely. Therefore, it is essential to recognize that our emotional health plays a very important role on our daily living.

Depending on the way that we feel emotionally, we react to the events and situations happening around us at that moment, during the day and in our lives. How we deal with a situation strongly depends on the emotional state we find ourselves at. In this regard, some people have developed a positive attitude and know how to handle situations in an objective way.

One of the questions we should ask ourselves is: How can I improve my emotional health so that I can build a better life for me? It is important to understand that in order to achieve this objective we must keep certain specific behaviors.

The first thing we should do is to avoid or remove all those things stealing our peace and making us feel bad, those things that are within your reach and that you can avoid. As an example, for starters, news are important, because they keep

us informed and updated, but it is not advisable to be focusing on the news all day, as they can be very depressing.

Social networks are like empty wagons, the greater noise they make, the emptier they are. In most social networks, people only publish what they want you to see; but not what they truly are, because they feel embarrassed of showing their failures or its common life similar to anyone else's. They make everyone else believe that they are living a fulfilled and happy life when in reality they are living an empty life full of routine and unhappiness.

How to maintain our mental health in an active and positive manner? There is nothing better than doing the things we love, and that can include physical activities. Sports are a valuable tool to prevent diseases such as diabetes and cardiovascular illnesses, among others, and they are also a way to stay active and positive.

Sharing with others, hanging out with our friends, or going to the movies together, getting a drink or dinner, helps us relax and release stress. Sharing time with someone special in order to quit our daily schedule helps us raise our mood and self-esteem.

Reading books, we like not only helps us grow as people, it also helps us in growing our minds. Because those who don't read, are only living one life: their own, a life full of limitations and lack of knowledge and information. Anyway, one thing we must be clear about is, we must do things and activities we enjoy, because that helps us improve our attitudes and our emotional states.

Your Mental Health

There are so many negative sources present in our daily life, from stress, anxiety, anguish and concerns to nervousness and dissatisfactions, among others. Knowing how to deal with all of these emotions is fundamental for mental health

One mentally healthy person can confront the challenges and day to day changes. You may recognize your limits and reach out for help whenever it is necessary.

How to stay mentally healthy on our daily activities?

In order to maintain a good mental health, it is necessary to take care of our bodies, this means sleeping well, eating correctly, and exercising in a constant manner. Physical activity is a great ally to mental health because it provides a feeling of wellbeing and relaxation.

When we exercise, our bodies release endorphins, a natural substance produced by the brain during and after physical activities. Releasing endorphins, also known as "the happiness hormones", helps us relax and reduce stress, as well as controlling anxiety, which contributes to the improvement of our mental health.

CHAPTER 5
YOUR PERSONAL RELATIONSHIPS

There are people with a huge ability to relate and maintain communication and conversations that make us have a good time. The gift of communicating opens a lot of great opportunities to establish healthy relationships with the right people in our personal or business life.

There are three types of relationships which directly influence our daily activities and everything we do: personal relations, which are the ones you maintain with your family and loved ones; social relations, which include your friends, and business relationships, related to your colleagues in work or business. Each of these play a definite role in our life and we approach each one of them differently.

The Mirror We Should Take a Look On

It doesn't matter if it is a personal or a business relationship; the way you look at yourself, is the way you will see other people. There comes the need to identify the type of mirror we use to evaluate ourselves. How we see ourselves, is how we will look at others. In consequence, it is necessary to evaluate ourselves within, if we wish to improve our relationships with others. If you are a negative person, you will look at the world in a negative way, but if you are a positive person, kind and loving, you will feel everyone else is too. The way your inner world portraits is the way your outside world will portray. This means your relationships with others will depend on this principle.

Your Couple's Relationship

To establish a good relationship, we must identify several factors which are essential for our relationship. Before relating to someone, you must know who you are. Recognizing who we are, is knowing what we can offer in a relationship. We must then understand and know what we want and expect to receive from our partners, in order to stay away from establishing a connection with the wrong person, meaning, with someone we have no affinity to.

It is important to remember that what you expect to receive from your partner, is nothing but a dream, a thought you have over what a relationship is, based on how you see yourself in the future. These are thoughts, not feelings. Affection, caring, and loving feelings arise after you treat each other. We can't confuse what we wish to accomplish with feelings, or vice versa.

Love

Is, without a doubt, one of the most meaningful characteristics in a relationship. It is a safe base for the beginning of a long and beautiful union, where we enjoy each moment and plan for a better future. Love helps us live in peace and harmony with that loved being God sent our way, to be our partner in life.

Love is the base of everything, it is the beginning and ending. We have been created by love; through love, we create a world full of possibilities where there are no barriers to reach our full potential with our loved ones.

Though the love you have for your partner, you will find motivation to grow as a person, and to improve yourself. Without noticing, love shapes us into a more loving, respectful, caring, and comprehensive person, to mention some characteristics. If we lack love, the relationship reaches a dead end, because that feeling is the core where the bond was created.

Therefore, knowing your own and your partner´s priorities will help you reach out and make better decisions and maintaining a better relationship, which, in turn, keeps the flame of love alive. Knowing your priorities and love language helps you define your strong points clearly, as well as your weak ones, in order to strengthen you core even more and work on strengthening the weak ones.

While you work on yourself, you must watch closely for your loved one´s priorities for love, so you can establish a good relation and have the same priorities language.

This is a very important detail, since couples go through different stages during their relationship.

The falling in love stage is the first one, this is where couples give their best to win and keep their partners happy; they both work hard to please the needs and desires of the other. This is the stage where everything is perfect since love seeks to overcome every inconvenience. This crush stage might last from two to three years, and then, we are on the second stage.

The complaints come with the second stage of the relationship; I call it, the whining stage, although this name appears to be sarcastic, since here – "watch out" – is where relationships go through serious challenges, where many

couples don't get to overcome their differences. Now is when certain behaviors begin to arise and certain attitudes don't go hand in hand with the couple's harmony. This second stage is when they actually begin to get to know each other, this is when he or she begin complaining about the lack of understanding, attention or help, since they are in a period when they handle too many responsibilities and commitments to fulfill everything they, probably, didn't even have before.

We find that, him not sharing time with her, not helping with the kids, or helping with home chores, giving enough attention or the consideration she deserves, is quite a common complaint at this point. In short, saying or complaining about endless things you can even imagine. While he answers back that he's been working all day so she and the kids have everything they need. If, at night, he wishes to be with her, he might find something like "I'm too tired", "let me sleep", and so they spend most of their time. She feels he is not considerate, and he feels rejected by her, which gives room for situations where the only result is creating an abyss between them.

Ignoring your couples' complaints is ignoring their requests. Although these requests are expressed in the form of complaint or whining, they don't cease to be requests that you both wish were taken care of. This is probably one of your love priorities, and, without knowing, you are both ignoring your spouse's love priorities, which leads to even more serious situations.

Ignoring your couple's requests is ignoring what is important to him or her, and this can affect the dynamic

between the both of you, up to the point where there is a huge gap about to destroy the relationship.

The best thing would be to talk about the subject and situations which are keeping you from understanding each other, so your differences may be solved. Ignoring your couples' complaints or requests will not only worsen your relationship, you will be telling your partner that you don't care about what he or she feels or thinks about it. When this happens, your couple finds that he or she is obliged to take on a similar attitude to yours in order to avoid more conflict between the both of you. This attitude will only worsen the situation since, an attitude as such, can only lead to a cold war.

The cold war is the third stage in a relationship, and it is the hardest of them all; this is when things have gone out of control; this is where one of them, or both, have a negative attitude towards the relationship. They are cold and distant, they have no considerations for their couple, and they seek reasons to not be around them. In the cold war, the conversations are minimum; they only talk when necessary and, when they do, it is because they have no other choice and they must talk about a specific subject, not to talk about them or the situation that is affecting their relationship.

At this stage, the person acts as if their couple does not care enough to be in the relationship and prefers to be alone. When these thoughts arise, the relationship is in grave danger, because one of them begins to act as if they were single, which may lead to a third party in the relationship, generating an even harder situation that will lead to misunderstanding.

Although at this cold war stage, both of them might still love each other, that does not mean the situation between them can't go worse; which is why it is of the most importance

to remember that, as time goes by, that dividing line gets bigger, wider and stronger, weakening the feelings and strengthening the resentment. While this happens, one or both of them will probably begin to look out to new horizons with the illusion of finding better opportunities outside the relationship.

We must avoid getting to that situation at all costs and do whatever it takes, to salvage the relationship. Communicating is very important but knowing how to listen to your partner is even more, since he or she is expressing how they feel about what is happening. When we listen to our partners and we act accordingly, we are letting them know how important they are for us.

This observation is relevant since your couple's relationship will depend on such. What you give and offer in a relationship is important but being responsible and fulfilling the duties and commitment of home, is your duty as a couple, partner, even if that doesn't mean either of you is happy.

What fulfills and makes your couple happy is when you do what he or she likes and loves, and vice versa, when they do what you like and love. Finding out what this principle is and carrying it out with love, will make you have a strong and happy relationship, because each one of you is fulfilling and complying with the needs and priorities your partner has, without ceasing to fulfill the responsibilities and duties of home or of your partner.

Not taking this principle into consideration and not carrying it out with love, and just doing it because you must, will not only jeopardize your relationship, but it will also affect the wellbeing of your physical, emotional, familiar, and economic health, as well as every aspect of yourself.

Here below, we will discuss some of the priorities to love, which are essential and which we must consider in order to maintain a happy and healthy couples' relationship. Remember that discovering your love priorities and your partners love priorities, to carry them out as much as possible, will help you maintain a healthy and strong relationship.

Respect

Is, without a doubt, a basic and necessary characteristic in the development of a healthy relationship. Respect draws a tight line which, if crossed inappropriately, might affect the relationship, because it involves feelings and emotions which are in constant battle with our actions and words.

If your partners love language or priority is respect, paying attention and listening to your partner when they are speaking to you, is a way of showing respect. There is a great difference between listening and hearing, since listening requires paying attention and acting in consequence when your partner speaks to you. The same thing happens when we see but don't observe. An observation requires or expects action from us. Maybe these details don't mean anything to you, but to him or her they might be of the outmost importance. Respect may be expressed though actions and gestures of kindness towards your couple. I recommend you read Matthew's biblical passage (13:10-17) found in page 41, once more.

Attention:

Is a gesture which plays a role of extreme importance in the social, business and, above all, in a couple's relationship environment. It is an attitude or action which does not require

anything from the party offering it but has unique value for those receiving it. It is treating your partner with commitment, showing with your actions that he or she is loved and appreciated. Is having that loved one present in certain details and in their needs.

Another way of attention is spending quality time with your partner, without being distracted or paying attention to things which are not him or her. Going out for dinner or talking a walk in the park to enjoy each other's company. Placing all your attention in them when they are speaking or when you are together, and not being distracted with social media or the phone or tv.

Attention is a general term, which has a different meaning for each person. Understanding what this means to you, will help you express your love language, while conscious or unconsciously, you let your partner know how you would like to be treated. It is essential to discover what this means for your partner, to be able to carry it out, since understanding their priorities and speaking their love language will keep them happy, and therefore, will contribute to having a healthy and solid relationship.

Words of Affirmation and Support

If your couple's love priority are the words of affirmation and support, you must provide them with positive words expressed with love and admiration towards them. These positive words may be compliments because of how they are or the way they behave around you. They are recognition or thank you words for what they do for you and others.

It is highlighting their virtues and admiring their qualities; it is expressing how thankful you are, with love and sincerity, because they are by your side.

Another way to express words of affirmation, is making your partner feel special, even when things are not working out for them. When those rough times arrive, let them know you are there to give them unconditional support. Give them words of encouragement when they need them most. Know your partner, so they can speak their love language and act in accordance with their love priorities.

Presents

If your partners love language is presents, going out for dinner or traveling, you may be sure that as long as you please them with a present, no matter how big or small it is, your partner will not only feel loved, but your relationship will be much better, because you will be speaking their love language. Same thing happens when you plan for vacations together or you surprise them, or when you make a dinner reservation, your couple feels loved and appreciated because you are responding to their love priorities. These are the reasons why knowing your partners priorities or love language is of main importance, so you can keep a healthy relationship.

Comprehension

Is putting yourself in another person's shoes, having empathy and seeing things from your partner's perspective. This gives them certainty that they are important in your life, because you value their point of view. Meaning, seeing things from the other person's perspective might help and increase

that tight line called respect and consideration which leads to a better relationship.

Another form of comprehension towards your couple is the act of service, helping your couple with the home chores. This love action may be expressed in different ways, whether that is taking care of the kids, going to the supermarket, taking out the trash, cleaning and loading gas for the car, or mowing the lawn. The act of service might be one of your couples' priorities when it comes to love.

It is your duty as a couple to communicate the priorities and love language to each other, since each one of you may speak or have a different love language. Knowing what this means and the importance it has for you, might be the difference between a happy and steady relationship or a difficult one. Remember that in order to harvest, we must first seed. If we want to harvest nice fruits, we must grow nice seeds, so our harvest is abundant.

Sexual Intimacy

This plays a determinant role in the relationship. Experts assure that the pleasure generated by this activity is of great help for the emotional and physical health within a couple.

However, and before anything else, it is essential to know what sexual intimacy means for each other in the relationship because, that way, you'll be able to speak the same language when it comes to sexual intimacy. Ignoring this principle or the importance of it, jeopardizes the relationship or the couple's stability.

Sexual intimacy flows in a transcendental manner because it is not just about the physical connection of the couple, it is also a connection representing the emotional side of the

relationship. In a determined moment, when love and passion meet at the same level, events and situations arise which go beyond imagination and activate endorphins, as well as the adrenaline.

The endorphins are chemical substances produced by the organism, which stimulate the brain areas where pleasant emotions are generated, making them key to the wellbeing and happiness. Endorphins allow you to feel pleasure and enjoy your couple.

Bed and Sex

If your couple's priority is sex, don't focus so much in luxury or details or going out for dinner and offering exquisite dishes or expensive gifts, because that is not their love language. Although your couple will accept and thank your good intentions, these will not have a greater impact, because you are not speaking their love language; they will just accept your gifts as a compliment.

To make your partner feel loved by you, your duty is to do whatever he or she likes when you are in bed or having sexual intimacy, since their love language is sex. When we do this for our couple, we are not just speaking their love language, but we are making him or her feel special.

Physical touch and the way we touch our partners is another way to show our love. This makes a huge difference for those individuals to whom love priority is sex. Touching certain parts of their bodies and doing it in a special way, according to their specific preference lets them know how important they are for you. Doing that for your partner is a way of keeping their love language full and satisfied.

Being creative and innovative in that aspect will strengthen your relationship. There are many ways to keep the relationship alive and there are different ways to do things, to keep the flame of passion alive. If you let your imagination and your partner's imagination fly with no prejudice, you will not only keep the relationship alive and active, but it will become stronger and healthier.

Isn't that what we really want to have in a couple's relationship? A healthy and strong relationship? If it is not with your couple, then, with whom? And if it is not now, when? Don't allow your limited way of thinking to be the reason for your unhappiness. There is an old saying that goes: "Don't leave for tomorrow, what you can do today".

There are so many ways to make the relationship flourish when passion begins to decrease, whether that is for health reasons or for circumstances and events which affect our daily lives. Therefore, it is important to seek some motivation to live new experiences in the sexual field. There are books and programs of self-help specialized in the subject, to keep and improve sexual intimacy between two people.

Agreeing on such subject is really helpful. Neglecting the relationship in this area might be a fatal mistake on many occasions because it allows for a space of confusion and sexual apathy, which will lead your partner to seek sexual exploration away from you. This will generate such serious issues that often end up with the termination of the relationship.

It is not about saying sex is the most important thing, but we must acknowledge that it does play a very important role in the relationship, unless there is an illness or physical impediment. For this reason, it is important to prioritize

sexual intimacy with your partner, to avoid unnecessary situations from affecting the relationship. If you lose sight of such significant details, your relationship will have ups and downs, probably more downs than ups.

Remember, you must know who and how you are, to know what you can offer to a relationship. Then, you need to know what you expect from your partner and the relationship; so this is a healthy and strong relationship. God's second commandment says: "You shall love your neighbor as yourself". Matthew (22:36-40).

> *36. Teacher, ¿which is the great commandment in the Law?*
>
> *37. Jesus said to him: You shall love the Lord your God with all your heart and with all your soul and with all your mind.*
>
> *38. This is first and greatest commandment.*
>
> *39. And the second is like it: You shall love your neighbor as yourself.*
>
> *40. On these two commandments hang all the Law and the Prophets.*

Meaning, are you loving your partner as he or she would like to be loved? Or how you would like him or her to love you?

Ask yourself:

Am I loving my partner as he or she would like to be loved?

Remember that if we wish to harvest, we must seed and grow.

How is your relationship at the moment?

How would you like it to be?

Why and with what end would you like to have a better relationship with your partner?

What can you do to improve your relationship?

How would you like your couple to treat you?

What can you do and how can you make it happen?

These are some of the questions we must ask ourselves if we wish to improve our couple's relationship.

Kids

Maintaining a good relationship with your partner will make your home a solid and safe place for all the members in your family. We must understand that the physical, mental, and emotional health of a kid depends, mostly, on the parents' stability. Therefore, it is of the outmost importance for parents that their children can grow in a safe and healthy environment, since, when problems arise in home, even kids end up in the middle.

The couples who maintain good communication between them, usually maintain a close relationship with their kids. Parents who talk more with their kids get to know them better, they get to know their interests and concerns.

These parents and kids relationship makes children get better grades and their school conduct be the correct one. It also helps them improve their emotional and intellectual development. At the same time, diminishes the risk of them falling in inappropriate conduct as smoking, drinking or having an addiction.

For that reason, it is important to establish a frequent dialog with your loved ones, to listen and understand their opinions, concerns, desires and needs. Good communication within a family serves as a base for a happy and responsible home, capable of solving differences between them effectively.

Ask yourself:

How is the relationship with your kids?

How would you like them to be?

Why would you like to have a good relationship with them?

What can you do to improve your relationship with them?

How would you like them to behave towards you?

What can you do and how can you help to make that happen?

These are a few of the questions we must ask ourselves if we wish to improve our relationships with our loved ones.

Social and Business Relationships

Interpersonal relationships consist in the interaction between two or more people. The ability to communicate, learn how to listen, how to solve conflicts and the way to do it, will determine your ability to establish good relationships.

The authentic portrayal of yourself will reflect the great human being you are to others and will allow for other skills to show in order to establish better relationships and opportunities.

It is of the most importance to remember that those who you choose to relate with daily, play a huge impact role over

your social, spiritual, and economic life. Your success depends on this on a great part, which is why it is determinant to know who we are relating with on a day to day basis. There are people who say we are the result of the five people we spend most of our time with. Ignoring these simple details can not only affect your life, but your present and future as well.

The relationships we establish with others play a basic role in our development and wellbeing. Through the same, we obtain important social and economic backup which favor our adaptation in the environment. Having the skills to establish correct relationships with others opens doors to many opportunities. On the contrary, the lack of such skills may cause difficulties on our personal, social and economic development.

It is important that we have knowledge, but it is more important to understand who we know, meaning, what influence we get from other people.

Therefore, knowing who we invest our time with will help us be more efficient in the development of projects and goals.

Take a moment and invest 15-20 minutes of your precious time to answer the following questions:

How can I improve my relationships with others?

Am I providing something valuable to others?

What knowledge, gifts, talents do I possess that can help me with my relationships with others?

Are the people around me on a daily basis providing something valuable into my life?

Are my fiends getting me to or away from my goals?

Do they have the same interests as I do to work together in a project?

What knowledge, gifts and talents do they possess that can help me reach my goals?

Do my friends influence me in a positive or negative way?

Is my social group providing value into my personal objectives?

CHAPTER 6: YOUR FINANCIAL GOALS

This is where we take Mark 10: 43 words as a starting point:

> *43. But it shall not be so among you. Instead, whoever desires to become great among you must be your servant and whoever wants to be first must be the slave of all.*

If you wish to be great and reach financial success, you must serve others. Yes, it is like that; just as you heard. You must be the most obedient among them, so you can listen and understand, to accept and act. You must be humble in heart, so you can have an open heart to learning. You must be the smallest one; the one who is willing to work hard and sacrifice for what you wish for, and for others, so, tomorrow, you can be the greatest. Because him who wishes to be great among you, must be the slave of all.

Don't go chasing money because money won't provide happiness. Do what you love and chase for success in that which you are passionate about, and so, money will follow. Yes, as such, and I'm going to say it again, don't chase money because money does not provide happiness. Do what you love to do and chase for success in everything you are passionate about, and money will follow. Focus on what you like to do, and you'll see what happens.

Your pattern for money

What is your pattern for money?

What does money mean to you?

Your financial future, dreams and projects will depend on the importance and value that money has for you. The concept you have about money plays a very important role in the fulfillment of your financial goals. If your pattern with money is that of prosperity, you have the possibility to reach the economic success you desire, but if your value over money is negative, you will probably live a life of failures and a lot of economic needs.

If you dream about having financial freedom, you must use every technique and tool necessary to make money come to you, because your income can only grow as much as you do. That's right: your financial pattern plays a fundamental role in the development and growth of your prosperity.

Have you heard about people who have obtained a lot of money in a very short amount of time and have economically collapsed in a short time as well?

Have you realized that there is people who have a lot of money and they lose it afterwards because of bad investments?

This has been seen with people who have won the lottery and, in the end, end up going back to their original economic state.

All of a sudden this appears to be bad luck or a bad move, but the truth is it is not like that. If one person receives an amount of money without being mentally prepared for it, it is most likely that they'll end up losing it.

However, those who have obtained money themselves, get the exact opposite results. When they lose their money, they generally get it back in a relatively short amount of time. Why? Because they might lose their money, but they never

lose the most important part that led to their success in the first place, their way of thinking, acting and their capacity to produce that money.

Your pattern with money is like a thermostat, which gets adjusted at the temperature you programmed it to. If your thermostat is programmed for a 70-degree temperature, and the temperature in the place went up to 85 degrees, or down to 55 degrees, then the thermostat would automatically adjust the temperature to 70. Why? Because it is programmed to do so at 70 degrees.

That is also the way your mind works, like a thermostat. If your financial mentality is programmed for a monthly or weekly income, you would find it hard to work on commission. The same thing happens when you are programmed to be an independent worker where you are the one controlling your income; working for a weekly or monthly paycheck would be hard. Therefore, it is of extreme importance that you recognize what is your financial mentality, because your life and your family's depend on it.

If you wish to change the results, you will have to modify your thoughts, because the point lies in your limited way of thinking and acting towards money. Your knowledge and strategies do not cease to grow. Your actions are the roots to your surroundings because everything you live and carry within you (in your being) is much more important than anything you see outside.

You may agree or disagree with me, but if you don't change your limited way of thinking, you won't be able to change your way of acting, which won't carry your knowledge, strategies or actions correctly, since you will be going against the laws of nature. Because everything that lies below ground,

creates what's above; what you are inside is shown on the outside as a reflection; everything visible reflects the invisible.

Your Income

Your income is as important as your spiritual, physical, mental/emotional, and familiar health.

Income plays a decisive role in our life since it helps us cover basic needs and satisfy other essential needs. It is also necessary to maintain a better quality of life and increase our economic development.

Acknowledging the importance of money helps us be aware of such, to be able to handle it correctly and use it correctly. Your income should be one of your five priorities, and you must take care of it as you take care of the others. If you know how to administer yourself and use good strategies, you will not only be able to reach your financial goals, you will also make your capital generate more income, and that way, you'll be able to improve your quality of life.

I believe that everyone, at some point in life, has wished for the financial freedom to do things we really like and get everything we desire. However, not everyone is willing to pay the price to have it. Although money does not buy happiness, it does provide us with a much better quality of life, being economically abundant and having less stress.

Your quality of life and the amount of money you can obtain will depend on your effort, and sacrifice. The bigger your desire of improvement, the greater the price to pay. In other words, your effort and sacrifice must be even greater. You must understand everything comes with a price, and nothing is free, but if we work hard enough, we can

accomplish our dreams and projects. I recommend you read, Sirach (6:18-37) the gift of knowledge and intelligence, once more, page 13.

What is the first thing you should know?

The first thing is reflecting on the following steps:

What do you wish to accomplish in terms of finance? Knowing what you want will help you get focused on what's important for you. For example:

What is the amount of money you would like to make on a monthly or weekly basis, by your work, business, or investments?

Second: Why and what for? Why is it important for you to obtain that amount of money?

What are the reasons motivating you to obtain that amount of money?

Make a list explaining what for and why would it be important for you to earn this sum of money. The more reasons you have, the stronger your "why", and this will give your life a bigger meaning.

Third: How? How will you accomplish what you want?

Develop a written plan of how you will accomplish it.

What will you do to earn such amount of money?

What are your plans and strategies to accomplish it?

Write everything down, step by step and with a lot of detail. If something doesn't work out, change the plan, but don't change the objective.

Fourth: When? When would you like to have or earn this amount of money or get to your objectives? Remember that if you do not date it, you'll probably never achieve it.

Fifth: Take action. Act and don't give up until you accomplish it. You must work on your goals and projects every day until they become a reality for you and a steady routine, so you can see your project develop day by day.

How to Create Goals

In the search for financial success, it is important to know exactly what we wish to accomplish, in order to take the necessary steps and reach and accomplish our dreams.

Knowing exactly what you want is the first step to achieve your objectives. This goal can be financial, meaning, certain amount of money you would like to earn or have. They can also be material things you would like to obtain, such as your dream house, a luxury car, etcetera. Regardless of your objectives, you must know exactly what you want. For example: if you wish to have a lot of money, don't go "I want to have a lot of money for this purpose". You must say the exact amount you need for this purpose, whether that is $50K or $100K, just say exactly how much you want. You must do the same thing with all your goals and objectives, naming each one of them.

Imagine for a moment that God chooses to grant you a lottery award of $5 million dollars so you can have and do everything you wish for the next 5 to 10 years. What would you do? Write in a blank page or in a diary, everything you would like to do or have, but that you haven't been able to because of the lack of money. Write everything down, leaving nothing out; imagine you just have one chance to do it.

Where would you like to go, whether that is alone or with the love of your life or your family?

What would you like to do?

What would you like to have?

A house, or a luxury car?

What would you do for others?

Would you help those in need?

Think about everything you would do if God granted you that miracle.

Luckily, God has already granted you that miracle. He placed gifts and talents into you by the Holy Spirit, which help you get his grace to lead a spiritual and personal life with wisdom and holiness. He placed those gifts and talents in you, but it is your responsibility and commitment to discover them and develop them to service others, in a way where you can improve your life and the world we are living in.

God sent Jesus to this world, his only child, to serve others, not to be served by us, and that's how God wants us to be with others. When we serve his people through the gifts and talents we have received, we are growing the seed of abundance and we will begin seeing the grace of God over us. He wants us to use our gifts and talents for our own benefit and the peoples' benefit, as well as to the honor and the glory of God.

It is important at this point to remember the talent parabola of Matthew (25: 14-30), which has already been quoted in page 49.

Having clear goals allows you to work with a fixed objective in mind, aside from working with more enthusiasm and harmony, since you have goals to fulfill. Knowing what you want allows you to prepare yourself psychologically to deal with events and situations which might happen during the process and help you prevent those situations from interrupting your dreams and projects. If you do not know what you want, God won't be able to help you either, because he who doesn't know where he is headed, ends nowhere.

Why and What for: Knowing why and what for is the second step in the road to fulfill our dreams and projects. As yourself why would you like to earn certain amount of money or

What are the reasons why you would like to accomplish those goals.

This gives you better clarity of motives to go after what you want. The why and the what for, are the engine that will keep the flame turned on when things get rough or when you feel like things don't go exactly how you want them to. If you don't have enough reasons pushing you forward, you are most likely to abandon your objectives upon the first challenge you face. So, the more reasons you have, the stronger the motivation.

Develop a plan to reach your objectives: Develop a written plan and strategize how you're getting there. Being an economically stable person requires clear and precise goals, if they are not clear, your decisions and actions won't be either. Therefore, it is fundamental that you take the corresponding time for good planning and carrying it out correctly.

Even more so, you must visualize yourself as a successful person. Those who really think that goals can be achieved, develop new skills and knowledge in the long term. Because, to reach our objectives, and the financial freedom we desire, our plans must be detailed and adequate.

Which strategy are you planning on using to achieve your objectives?

Who are your allies or partners? Who are you counting on to achieve your objectives?

How much time will you have to invest and for how long?

What amount of money will you have to invest and for how long?

Think about everything that might help you develop a good plan to be successful.

Date it: You must know when you would like to achieve your goals. Having an objective is important, and knowing the why is even more important, but, if you don't date it, you'll probably never get there. Therefore, it is important to set a definite time frame to achieve your goals. This will help you stay focused and prioritize correctly. Otherwise, you won't be able to grant your purpose the necessary time or attention. Postponing this action is just postponing achievements in your life.

Taking action: you must act until you reach your objectives. This is a must, if we don't act, everything else is just worthless. One goal, as developed as it is, requires actions to achieve the desired objective. Those who wish to reach financial success don't have any kind of excuse. They are driven by their passion because they surround themselves with positive people, who have one same vision.

How to Manage Your Finances

Administering your finance in an efficient and responsible manner is as important as the amount of money we earn because our quality of life and heritage we create for the future depends on this. A good management of the money will help us achieve a better economic future, and, at the same time, reach other objectives both in the long and short term, such as holidays, going out on vacation, buying a house or a new car, among others.

There is the myth that economically successful people have a natural gift for handling their finances, but this is not true. To build wealth for ourselves we require effort and sacrifice, discipline, and persistence, but, above all, time and a strategic plan which is well developed. We must recognize that everything we want and worth having requires dedication and effort and sacrifice, a series of guidelines to expose:

Effort: You must work hard and set clear, ordered priorities. Knowing the difference between wanting something and needing something will help you make better financial decisions and not do impulse buying.

Sacrifice: Choosing between one thing and another (wanting or needing) will be necessary, understanding needs are more important than pleasure. We cannot have everything we want at the same time, so you will have to sacrifice one thing over the other.

Effective action: Handle your finances correctly, and always do the right thing, so you don't have to look back with sorrow. Remember that your thoughts provide feelings. Feelings lead into action. Actions provide results.

Discipline: Is doing what you don't want to do but is good for you.

Develop unbreakable discipline, where effort, sacrifice, action, persistence, and character, play a very important role in the search for your dreams and projects, in a way you can make good decisions when you need to.

Persistence: This characteristic does not know defeat or failure. Which is why you must understand that, in order to maintain certain level of quality of life and create wealth and heritage for the future, you must be persistent, because that is what keeps us focused on our purpose.

Development of a Financial Plan

A financial plan is like a GPS which tells you exactly where you are, where you want to go, how to get to your final destination, at the right time. If you make a mistake and take the wrong path, the GPS will automatically pull you out and place you in the right direction so you can reach your final destination at the right time.

We must also have a financial plan which allows us to look at our current economic situation and develop a plan for the future which will help us reach our financial goals at the right time. Not having a well-developed financial plan is like driving from New York to Florida without a GPS or a map to guide us. We will most likely get lost in the way and we will never get to our final destination, or we will waste time turning without direction.

That is what happens when you work without a financial plan. As hard as you try, you won't be able to execute your decisions correctly, which will jeopardize all your goals and delay your success, or, even worse, not lead you to your

desired objectives. Therefore, working with a budget or a financial plan is a must, to make your dreams and projects come true.

A financial plan must take your income, savings, expenses and debts into consideration, as well as a short and long term projection for the future.

Your income: Is the money you receive on a yearly or monthly basis. This money can be from your work, business or investments and you need it to cover for basic needs.

Your savings: Is an amount of money that you take from the income, to save, on a monthly or yearly basis with the sole purpose of having a savings fund and short and long term investments or for future purchases. These savings can be between 20-40% of your income, depending on your needs.

Your savings must include several accounts: one savings account for retirement, where you save up a 10% of your income. An emergencies account of 3-6 months of your monthly expenses. Another savings account for education, so you can improve your knowledge and income. One more for personal needs. These accounts must be fully separated, because each one of them plays a different role in terms of finance.

Your expenses: Means the money we have, to cover for basic needs of life from food, clothes, rent, vehicle expenses, and other inevitable situations. If you know how to administer yourself, these expenses cannot go over 60-70% of your income. Otherwise, you'll be living way above your budget, which will jeopardize your economic health both in the present as in the future.

Your debts: If you have debts, make up a plan to pay for all of them, as soon as possible. Begin by making a list (credit cards, car loans, educational credits, etc.). Include the actual balance, minimum payment by month, and interest. Afterwards, check your budget to determine how much more you can add to the payment of your debts so you can get out of them as soon as possible. Take a closer look at everything you're paying monthly; this is money you can save every month for more important things that will improve your quality of life or work for short or long term investments.

If you develop a plan and follow it exactly how you developed it, taking this advice into consideration and acting with discipline and the necessary persistence, I can assure you, you will not only get out of the depts, you will also be able to achieve your financial goals. Actually, if you consider these recommendations, you will begin to grow the seed of abundance and will be on the path to success. That's how Matthew (25: 21) said it, and we say it again:

> 21. His master said to him: 'Well done, good and faithful servant. You have been faithful over a little; I will set you over much. Enter into the joy of your master.

However it is, remember that even if you have a defined plan, it won't work if you lack action, effort, sacrifice, discipline and persistence. All your efforts will be in vain because your gifts and talents will be buried underground for the fear of failure or because you were lazy, just like the one who got a talent and wasted it, quoted in Matthew (25:24-30) talents, on page 49.

I hope this advice can help in achieving your objectives with certainty and clearly. If you must seek for someone's' help who has the necessary knowledge to guide you through the whole process, do it, it will be of great help. Remember we all need a guidance (a coach), someone to help us get oriented step by step to achieve our goals or, at least, to help us, until we can do it for ourselves.

CHAPTER 7
HOW AM I?

Assess your personality, so you can grow more each day

Your Character

Character is made up by the particular things describing how you are. We say someone has character when a person develops virtues and qualities that make them different from others. Generally, they are determined, capable of distinguishing between good and evil, fair and unfair, correct and incorrect. They stand strong and steady; they don't let themselves be intimidated easily upon the circumstances and injustice of men. They can assume their responsibilities and accept the results objectively.

In such away, people with character usually face a lot of opposition because they are doing the right thing based on their values and principles, and not for bias or favoritism. They are worthy people to have around because they offer a true friendship. In terms of work or business, those who recognize the value and importance of these people will want to have them in their work team or as partners in a company, because they will seek the good interests of the company and not their own.

Although attitude and character are very similar, we can notice that character is based on the way you are, through virtues and qualities which lead to act or think in a determined way. On the other hand, attitude is about developed behavior by events or situations, which lead to act and think in a certain way, whether that is positive or

negative, in accordance to how you manage the experience you are living.

Your Attitude

Why is it important to have a good attitude or positive attitude?

Attitude is developed by events and situations which are happening to us and transforming into feelings. Attitude may be the result of lived experiences, whether that is personally or by a foreign situation, meaning, situations that have happened to other people which lead us to develop a positive or negative feeling about what happened.

There are people capable of recognizing good attitude from others just by watching their behavior and establishing a conversation with them, while others have a huge ability to relate to people and maintain a nice communication.

However, there is other people who have a terrible attitude to relate to others. We find these individuals daily, on the streets, work and in our own families as well. These situations happen every day between the people close to us and the place we work at. These are people dedicated to creating bad situations wherever they go.

This type of people go around the world growing and harvesting problems and discussions. If you let yourself be dragged by them, they will tighten up your environment. They live criticizing and diminishing your virtues and qualities, as well as highlighting your flaws to others, without noticing the problem is actually them. The best you can do is stay away and as far as you can from people like that because their presence darkens the environment. Some of them lack

scrupulous and are capable of treating others in a bad manner without any remorse.

If you feel like you need to change your attitude, you would be better recognizing clearly what it is that you must change. Look, nowadays, having a good attitude can open social and business opportunities. Therefore, performing an honest and detailed evaluation on the negative traits you must improve or change, is a need.

Evaluate your reasons and the why you should improve your attitude. Ask yourself: How has my attitude affected my personal and economic relationships? What are my reasons to change? Your ability to change will depend on your motivation to do so; therefore, you must have very good reasons to achieve it. Never allow a bad attitude to be an obstacle in your personal life and in your business success.

Your Self-Esteem

Having a high self-esteem is essential for the physical, spiritual, mental/emotional and economic development of the individual. Feeling confident in oneself, capable of confronting every adversity of life. Feeling accepted by ourselves. A positive self-esteem allows us to face life with greater optimism and confidence, and, therefore, reach our desired objectives easily.

Your self-esteem is an evaluation of yourself which allows you to take a different look at life and at the world, according to your optimism. If you lack self-esteem, you will see life in a negative way and will have a lot of difficulties to achieve your objectives, meaning a constant struggle, like swimming against the current.

People with a high and positive self-esteem tend to have a good attitude, which allows them to develop new skills to face every upcoming difficulty and challenge.

An optimistic person feels satisfied and fulfilled, capable of reaching the desired objectives. Such virtue turns out to be extremely important in the business world, since it highlights one person over those who lack of it.

Without a doubt, this is one of the most important qualities that one person can have, because on it, depends how we see ourselves within and how we see the outside world. We must not forget that whatever we feel on the inside, we reflect on the outside.

If we are aware of the importance of self-esteem, we will realize it plays a fundamental role in our lives and, our future depends on it. Which is why I am asking these questions:

How do you describe yourself?

Are you a negative or a positive person?

How do you feel when your self-esteem is high?

What can you do to improve your self-esteem?

Remember: your self-esteem is how you see yourself, and so will you see the world around you.

Your Optimism

Being optimistic helps us look at life in a positive way. Thanks to this characteristic we seek for possibilities in each situation, to reach our goals. An optimist will always get something positive from a negative situation. The optimist sees the glass as half full, while the pessimist sees it half

empty. Any of the two options are correct. The difference lies in the point of view and where it leads.

If you are an optimist, you'll see life in a positive way. Seeing the glass half full, will make you seek for all the possibilities to finish filling it. Meaning, the optimist seeks for and finds a way to turn the negative into positive, turning the invisible into visible.

An optimist must be objective, knowing why the desired goal is important and how it can be achieved. This probably means getting out of your comfort zone, to think and act outside your objectives, which will take a lot of effort and sacrifice from you, to reach your goals, as mentioned.

It is important to take risks, but calculated ones. Our goals must be planned objectively, studying the pros and cons before carrying out the plans to avoid disappointment along the way. We cannot allow our optimism to blind us because this would lead us to a state of failure which would have a negative impact on our lives.

Do you feel like you're an optimist or do you think you have to work more on it?

How has being an optimist helped you? If you are not, how do you think you can improve your way of thinking?

Do you think the way you think, and act has helped you reach your objectives?

If you were an optimist, do you think your personal or economic situation today would be different?

CHAPTER 8
PAY THE PRICE FOR SUCCESS

Commit Yourself to Success

We all have dreams and goals that we want to achieve. Dreaming about them is escaping reality and sailing, for an instant, towards the future we wish to live in. These dreams and projects are the engine that pushes us towards a better and filled with purpose life. Recognizing our objectives is important but recognizing those obstacles which prevent us from reaching them, is even more important because that is what helps us work in our weaknesses. Therefore, we must know what the price is, and we must be willing to pay it, if we truly want to achieve our dreams. We cannot allow any obstacles, big or small, to stop us.

With this purpose in mind, we must understand that dreams require three things from you: the change you must make in yourself, the time you must invest, and the money you'll have to spend to achieve what you want.

The change: Is the adjustment you need to make in yourself to achieve your dreams. You must change your limited way of thinking, so you can change your way of acting. Remember that your thoughts provide feelings, your feelings lead into action, and your action provides results.

Time: Is the time you'll have to invest to achieve your dreams. The days, months and years you have to dedicate to this sole purpose. Dreams require a lot of effort and sacrifice, but above all, a lot of time.

Money: Is the amount of economic resources you'll have to invest to make whatever you wish for, a reality.

To achieve your dreams, each of the next three points is necessary.

If you don't take care of them all, you'll probably never achieve what you wish for. Trying to achieve your dreams without making a change, investing the time and money required, would be like going against the natural laws of life. As much as you try to, you won't get far, and if you do, you'll have paid a much higher price to reach your goal, which is why I don't recommend it. What I do recommend is paying attention to the details I'm about to mention.

The Cost of Change

Changing is being reborn in Spirit, so you can leave all your prejudice behind and start over with no fear. Leaving all your limitations and negative beliefs behind, so you can act in a positive way. Transforming yourself firmly and steadily, not interrupting the greatness of the Lord with your small concerns.

Let's see what John (3:1-7) has to say about his:

> *Now there was a Pharisee, a man named Nicodemus, who was a member of the Jewish ruling council. He came to Jesus at night and said: "Rabbi, we know that you are a teacher who has come from God. For no one could perform the things you are doing if God were not with him.*

> *Jesus replied: «Very truly I tell you, no one can see the Kingdom of God unless they are born again.»*
>
> *Nicodemus asked: "How can someone be born when they are old? Surely, they cannot enter a second time into their mother's womb to be born."*
>
> *Jesus answered: «Very truly I tell you," No one can enter the Kingdom of God, unless they are born with water and the Spirit.*
>
> *Flesh gives birth to flesh, but the Spirit gives birth to spirit.*
>
> *You should not be surprised at my saying: You must be born again".*

The Price of change is paid by leaving behind all the bad habits that are keeping you away from your dreams, since they are not according to God's principles or the principles of success. These bad habits and beliefs have kept you away from the grace of God because they are limiting your spiritual and intellectual capacity, keeping you from reaching success and your highest potential.

If we are not where we wish we were, or we don't have what we would like to have, it is because we are not doing what we should be doing. I'm going to repeat myself: Our limited way of thinking and acting does not match what the Lord has prepared for us, or with success. This negative way of thinking and acting keeps us from growing to a much higher level.

We all have certain habits that have influenced us negatively, to the point where they lead to failure. In most cases, these negative habits have been developed since we

were little; these are behaviors, attitudes, and actions, often conscious ones, although in some cases they are completely unconscious. It is of the outmost importance that we recognize these conducts so we can make the necessary changes.

One more detail to remember: Although the time and money we invest to achieve our dreams is mandatory, if you strive away from God's grace, you will be drifting away in an un-sailed ship with no direction.

In conclusion, if we don't change our limited way of thinking and acting, our efforts will be in vain and won't give us full satisfaction. Which is why we must develop new habits, according to God's will, and with the principles of success, otherwise, we will pay the price of not doing it, for staying on unsafe ground.

The Cost of Regret

Now we will be discussing some of the main causes which keep us from reaching or highest potential and away from our dreams.

Ignoring the importance of what we are about to talk next is keeping yourself from the grace of God, forgetting that this is the main base to reach the success we desire, whether that is spiritual, physical, emotional, familiar, or economic.

Are you ready to make the change? Let's begin!

To trace a path which will lead to change, we must clarify some concepts:

Contrast between Disobedience and Obedience

Disobedience is an act of denial, not understanding, embracing, or abiding by the rules. It is a resistance towards authority or going against norms and established regulations. It is being undisciplined, with no respect to an established work frame. It is going against God's will and his principles, just because we are following our own desires. Those actions of disobedience are condemned by God.

The disobedient one thinks and acts differently, and that makes adapting for the fulfillment of his obligations or work, hard.

Disobedience is shown since an early age, around two years of age, when children begin to have the first signs of personality and self-discovery. This is the way they learn and discover their own paths. As they grow, the acquire more knowledge, and so they should also discover their parent's rules and other signs of authority, because that is where we begin to form a line for their teenage years and adult life.

The Bible tells us about great men who suffered the consequences of their disobedience. Moises was banned from the promised land. Saul lost the kingdom God had given him. Samson lost, not only his strength, but his life.

David was betrayed by one of his children and some of his ranking officers, who tried to take his life. Lot's wife became a salt statue. The prodigal son experienced the tough consequences of his disobedience; his ruin was great, his misery was as well, up until he wished to be able to eat pigs food to survive.

On the other hand, obedience cares for the opposite. Delivering yourself to the will of God because He loves the

obedient and humble by heart. Without a doubt, obedience stands out as one of the most important virtues in a human being. Those who possess it, carry the seed of abundance with them, since obedience is accompanied by a lot of virtues and qualities, possessed by a few, and they keep the person on track.

Obedience is paying attention, with humility. It is listening with an open heart with no prejudice or resentment. Understanding what we are being told peacefully and with harmony. Accepting with humility so we can act with faith, believing everything is going to be okay. Accepting that God is in control, and He wants what's best for us.

In Luke (5:4-6) obedience is illustrated, overcoming even what logic would assume:

> *4. When he had finished speaking, he said to Simon: Launch out into deep and let down the nets for a catch.*
>
> *5. Simon answered: 'Master, we've toiled all night, and caught nothing; nevertheless, at Your word, I will let down the nets.'*
>
> *6. And so they did, and caught such a large number of fish, that their nets began to break.*

Obedience is trusting and believing in the Lord, without having seen first. Walt Disney, the creator for one of the largest amusement parks in the world, despite every difficulty, trusted and believed in his project. Although Disney passed away shortly before the park was finished, today, millions of people around the world get to see and enjoy the park, because he saw it first through faith. And if

this example is based on a human fact, how much more will we see if we trust the Creator.

Obedience is giving without expecting anything in return, acting with no guarantees, investing your time without watching out for the clock, recognizing the difference between having to do something or wanting to do something, doing what we must even if we don't like it, delivering yourself, fully, if you truly wish to receive the blessing God has prepared for you.

If you don't surrender to obedience and humility, you'll live a life full of struggle, bitterness, frustration and suffering, pain, and sadness. The worst part is your children will suffer the consequences too, because, without noticing, you will seed and grown misfortune in them, since it is impossible to give what we don't have and teach what we don't know. That is the explanation to understand why obedience is one of the most important qualities you can have in life. I recommend you read Sirach (6: 18-37) on page 13.

Love

Love is the first and second commandment of God. Love everything you do, no matter how big or small your dream and project. Love and honor your job or business, because he who does not honor little, cannot be honored with more. Don't do things just because you must; when you do something, do it with love, because if it is not done like this, your facts will give you away. That is what Matthew meant in (7:15-20):

> *A Tree and Its Fruit*
>
> *15. Beware of false prophets, who come to you in sheep's clothing, but inwardly are ravenous wolves.*
>
> *16. You will recognize them by their fruit. Are grapes gathered from thornbushes, or figs from thistles?*
>
> *17. So, every healthy tree bears good fruit, but the diseased tree bears bad fruit.*
>
> *18. A healthy tree cannot bear bad fruit, nor can a diseased tree bear good fruit.*
>
> *19. Every tree that does not bear good fruit is cut down and thrown into the fire.*
>
> *20. Thus you will recognize them by their fruit.*

Procrastination

Is postponing the action, the habit of delaying activities or situations that must take place. Is not executing an action, whether by fear or laziness. This kind of behavior and action turns the person into a slacker, to God, a sinner. The lazy develops a negative and comfort attitude, leaving everything for later, and God abhors that type of behavior.

The Gospel of Matthew (25:1-13) tells us about this topic in the Parable of the Ten Virgins:

> *1. Then, the kingdom of heaven will be like ten virgins who took their lamps and went to meet the bridegroom.*

2. Five of them were foolish, five of them were wise.

3. For when the foolish took their lamps, they took no oil with them.

4. But the wise took flasks of oil with their lamps.

5. As the bridegroom was delayed, they all became drowsy and slept.

6. But at midnight there was a cry: 'Here is the bridegroom! Come out to meet him!'

7. Then all those virgins rose and trimmed their lamps.

8. And the foolish said to the wise: 'Give us some of your oil, for our lamps are going out.

9. The wise answered saying: 'Since there will not be enough for us and for you, go rather to the dealers and buy for yourselves.

10. And while they were going to buy, the bridegroom came, and those who were ready went in with him to the marriage feast, and the door was shut.

11. Afterward the other virgins came also, saying: 'Lord, Lord, open to us.

12. But he answered: 'Truly, I say to you, I do not know you.

13. Watch therefore, for you know neither the day nor the hour.

The Lord is reminding us that, if we wish to feast on his dwelling, and reach our highest potential here on earth, we must be spiritually prepared and intellectually capable to

receive the blessings He has saved for us, since we do not know when those blessings or his arrival will come.

Commit to Action

The opposite to laziness is action, which shows commitment to change, to take the path towards prosperity, both spiritually and personally. I imagine that, by now, you already know what you wish to accomplish, because you have gotten here reading this book. If so, it is time to commit and act, immediately. A lot of the people who purchase a book or go through a self-help course, don't even get to read the second chapter, or don't take the necessary actions to obtain the desired results. Commitment and action are the price to change, acting and doing things differently; with love and commitment, if you wish to obtain different results. To explain it better, we have Matthew's Parable of talents (25:14-30), which we have already quoted in page 49. Complimenting what was said in that quote, it is good to mention that your path to prosperity, and the action you develop in it, will have encouraging and discouraging moments and aspects.

Faith

All who wish to achieve their dreams, must maintain unbreakable faith, because faith is the only thing that can turn the invisible into visible, impossible into possible. Faith is the engine that powers us to keep going, even when things don't go right or the way we want them to. A touching example is provided by Centurion when he asks Jesus to heal Matthew (8:9-13). As we stated on page 47, this roman officer believed so deeply, that he was only to ask for the Word of Jesus for a miracle to happen.

Attitude

Bad attitudes arise due to events or situations which happen and burden us with a negative load, but, regardless of the reason, we must get over it and maintain an appropriate attitude, which will open doors to opportunities in the business and social world. It is of the outmost importance to keep and maintain a good attitude if we wish to reach our highest potential and achieve our goals.

Fear:

Fear is a phenomenon which destroys you day by day. Being a prisoner of your own feelings, is hushing your voice and killing your dreams. Fear takes the pleasure away of everything that's possible. It is a silenced cancer which destroys you within.

It is worse than death, because fear kills you every day, while death kills you only once. Fear is the product of the lack of information and knowledge, fear of failing, and what everyone else will say, fear to what others might think of you and to the unknown.

At times, it is convenient to be a little scared, because it protects us from danger, but we cannot have paralyzing fear. I believe every single one of us, at some point of our lives, has gone through an emotionally insecure phase of our lives. It is something that affects us all, and it usually comes from the lack of trust in oneself or the lack of character. He who lacks personality or character, is at the mercy of low self-esteem and vulnerability to others.

Why should we face fear? Because that is the only way we will be able to experience the desired freedom and reach our highest potential, the one we were created for. Something to stand out is that fear is not overcome, it is just faced according to the situation we are dealing with. Fear is an automatic mechanism of the human being, which activates when we recognize something is not quite right, and so, it protects us from danger. Therefore, we can only handle it in each situation we face.

To not be stuck, you just must face it; take and act as necessary until you get past that situation. Movement towards a new opportunity helps you confront fear. Another way to do it, is reading self-help books and socializing, especially with people in the area you wish to surround yourself with. That way you'll be able to increase your confidence and your presence. When you handle fear, you feel free, to look at a world full of possibilities and new opportunities.

The moment we understand fear is the main weapon to kill our dreams, we can be prepared to face it, working objectively without ignoring the risks of doing it.

Pessimism

The pessimist has the tendency to see the worst part of every situation. That negative attitude comes from our limited way of thinking and acting. As the saying goes, he who does not read; does not grow, and he who doesn't grow; lives but one life: his own. A life full of limitations by a narrow way of thinking, caused by the lack of information and knowledge. The pessimist sees the glass as half empty, although it is also half full. It is not the situation affecting the pessimist, it is the

way he or she sees the situation, which will lead him or her to act according to his thoughts.

Be an Optimist

If you are a pessimist, you need to change the way you think, so you can change the way you act, but do it now. Change your paradigm and adopt a new vision of optimism, so you can seed and grow abundance in yourself and not allow your limited way of thinking to be the cause of misfortune.

Impatience Against Patience:

Impatience is a deeply ingrained evil which we all carry within us and destroys everything that would be possible if we just dedicated the necessary time to everything we wish for. Not recognizing the value of things or the importance of time. We diminish the importance of time, and without noticing, cease the acts and blessings that God has for each one of us. Ignoring and denying that God's time is perfect, that your dreams and projects won't come a minute, not even a second later than expected.

On the other hand, patience helps us understand the setbacks and difficulties, to obtain what we want. Patience is to be able to understand that everything is a process and that, though time, we will discover the necessary steps towards our objectives. According to this idea, Matthew's quote is highly appropriate (5:5):

> 5. Blessed are the meek for they will inherit the earth.

Discipline

Is a very determinant characteristic for human beings. Those who possess it, have other virtues and qualities as well, which make them stand out from the rest. They acknowledge their virtues and qualities and develop them, but also know how to recognize their weaknesses, and work on them.

People with a high level of discipline understand the difference between having to do something and wanting to do something. They recognize that discipline is not only about doing what they want to do, but doing what they must do, even if they don't like it.

All the principles here stated, are of high priority for the achievement of dreams, but, without a doubt, discipline is at the top. He who enjoys a high level of discipline, possesses many of the previously mentioned principles and will enjoy a superior quality of life over others, because it has grown the seed of abundance in himself.

Persistence

Persistence is, without a doubt, another essential characteristic we need to have if we want to achieve our goals and projects. All the qualities here mentioned make up persistence, meaning, men and women who possess these qualities are called upon success.

When we balance it, we see that persistence is the product of effort and sacrifice which has sustained over time. It means focusing every day on achieving our objectives, even when we know we are sacrificing something. It is recognizing why our dreams and projects are important to us. It is not giving up, as

hard as overcoming our obstacles gets. Persistence does not know failure or listens to the words "I can't".

In other words, persistence is the sum of virtues and qualities working for one same purpose. It is like your body, made up of organs and different body parts, but part of one same organism. Although. Each part works differently, they all benefit the same body. That's also how virtues and qualities work when we develop them.

If you do not apply persistence, your dreams and projects are in grave danger of never coming to be, since you have not made up a long-term vision. It is important to remember that, when we are persistent, we are evolving the different gifts and talents God has placed upon each one of us, to be developed and placed to work in the service of others. With these gifts and talents, we reach our dreams and projects, reflecting the blessings God has for us, and the greatness and mercy of our Lord.

The Price of Time

Time is a Price we must pay if we wish to achieve our dreams. If there is anything in this life that we cannot change, rewind, extend, or purchase, is time. Time is a gift from God, and although we all have the same number of hours in one day, not all of us get the same amount of time to achieve and enjoy our goals. Time is a treasure, and he who does not value it, loses it.

If you wish to achieve your goals and dreams, you'll have to invest time properly; knowing your dreams and projects require a lot of effort and sacrifice. Therefore, knowing the difference between quantity of time and quality of time, is very important. Knowing that being very busy does not mean

going forward; that working a lot, does not mean accomplishing much. Knowing your decisions and priorities must be clear and precise so your actions are as well. Is working correctly so you don't spend your time inappropriately and invest it correctly.

Work with the rule 80-20 so you can use your time properly and be able to achieve your objectives in the least time possible. This rule says the following: 80% of your daily activities will only give you 20% of the desired results which led to your dreams, while 20% of your daily activities will provide 80% of your dreams.

What does that mean to you? It means you are probably investing time in less important activities, which have no greater impact in the results you wish to obtain. Focus all your effort in the 20% of the activities which will provide 80% of the desired results. Knowing how to invest your time efficiently and properly, we will make a great difference in the projects and objectives you wish to achieve.

The Price of Money

Money is another important element in the achievement of your dreams. Every dream requires time, but money as well, and this is a price we all must pay. There are two kinds of investments: First, the capital you need to invest to train and acquire knowledge. Second, the capital you need to invest for your dream.

The Price of Training and Knowledge

This means investing your time and money to learn everything you need about that thing you want to exercise. It is going to college if whatever you desire requires a title or a

degree. It is taking online lessons or a training course to be able to perform in whatever field you desire. Investing in books and seminars to be able to be a professional in the subject you wish to be. Having someone, whether that is a teacher or an instructor, to help you and guide you step-by-step in the realization of your dreams. I recommend you go back to the quote, "the Gift of Knowledge and Intelligence", Sirach (6: 18-37), page 13.

The Price of Your Dream

Is the capital you have to invest to acquire that which you desire, weather that is setting up a business, a company, or even traveling. It is the sum of the money that you need to invest in order to grant life to the dream you so much desire to achieve, that which gives meaning to your life.

Unfortunately, a lot of people invest great sums of money in that which they wish to do or have, without having invested in the necessary time to get knowledge and the required preparation to achieve their desires. Therefore, I recommend investing in yourself first, learning everything you need to, inform yourself and educate yourself in the field where you wish to practice, before you invest capital, so in the end, you don't end up wasting time and money.

CONCLUSION

The purpose of this book is to bring value into your life, and at the same time, help you set clear priorities and order the magnitude of each of them, so you can live a full life and you can get to reach your maximum potential in each of the stages and steps mentioned. Understanding the importance of this priorities and living in accordance with his principles, will not only bring you spiritual, physical, emotional, familiar, and economic stability, it will also influence the harmony of your home, in a way that you will be happier amongst your own.

Nowadays we live in a world that is so complex and changes so quickly that, if we don't have our priorities in order, we will easily lose ourselves in the social and economic environment surrounding us, as well as in trouble and situations that are exhausting and present every day. Recognizing and acknowledging our priorities and setting them in order and by meaning will not only give us emotional stability, but it will also help us make better decisions in our lives, especially in decisive moments where we tend to choose between one priority and another.

I remember one time, when COVID-19 pandemic was at a very high-level in New York City. Genesis, one of my daughters, with only 13 years of age, asked me: "Daddy, I know you have to go to work, but are you going out in the middle of this pandemic?" I could sense worry and anguish for me in her voice. So, I told her: "Baby, you know my priorities, don't you? Between health and work or money, health comes first". Listening to those words I was able to feel

a change inside her, I noticed that her face changed when I told her I wasn't going out.

Maybe you or someone you know has taken bad decisions because they haven't had their priorities in order. We know of people who have lost their health just because they wanted to make money, to then lose their money trying to gain back health, and in the end, they didn't enjoy any of them.

Others have lost their families and loved ones because they dedicated all their time into work, ignoring that love and attention were more important to their families than the luxuries or things they could offer, and without noticing, they abandoned or didn't take care of their families both physically and emotionally. So I ask you, what good does it do to achieve your objectives if, in the end, you don't have your loved ones to enjoy them with?

Others have sacrificed her life or their freedom because they were doing illegal things just to obtain an acquire wealth, in such a way that they ended up losing their own lives trying, while others lost their wealth trying to gain back freedom. In the end, they end up losing everything: their lives, their freedom, and their money.

These individuals have wanted what's best for themselves and for their families, but conscious or unconsciously they have not taken care of things in a matter of priorities. Although intentions have been good, decisions have been bad, and for many, decisions and results have been fatal. This is a price to pay which I don't wish or recommend upon anyone.

When I was writing this book, I was thinking about all those young people who are in school, or high school, and

those who are already in college getting ready to start a new stage in their lives. I was thinking about how these principles might help them make better decisions from the start of their youth.

While I was writing the book, I was also thinking about all the couples going through difficult times in their marriages, just because they haven't been able to understand basic needs and the priorities of their spouse within the relationship. Whether that is a lack of interest or lack of information or knowledge, this situation will only worsen the relationship further, creating complications between them. My objective is to provide a small step so they can overcome their differences and make their homes a happy place with new hopes and possibilities, along with new opportunities for them and their families.

My greatest wish is to be able to help you, and I really believe that the concepts within this book may help you change your life, and your families' lives radically if you just wish so. If you commit to using these principles and making them part of your daily life, you'll begin seeing changes in your life from the start. Your thoughts and actions will no longer be the same and, therefore, your results will be different.

I would even love to be able to deliver this book personally to give you a little push towards the steps that will lead you into changing your life, since I wrote it thinking about you. If the principles contained within these pages bring any value into your existence, I would like that, aside from making them part from your daily lives, you could share them and give her a copy of the book to your loved ones or to anyone who needs it, so they can benefit from it as well.

I firmly believe that, together, we can make a huge difference in the lives of our children, spouses, brothers and sisters, friends, and family. We can all bring something in many aspects, so that our lives and our families lives improve, and so we can live in happy homes, filled with new horizons.

BIBLIOGRAPHY

Latin American Bible in Spanish. (1995).

https://www.bibliatodo.com/la biblia/version/Latinoamericana-1995